(in HB for)
43.-

MUSIC

THE

NATIONAL MUSIC OF AMERICA

AND ITS SOURCES

The National Music of America

And Its Sources

By
Louis C. Elson

Author of "Curiosities of Music," "European Reminiscences," "The Theory of Music," "Great Composers and Their Work," etc.

ILLUSTRATED

Boston

L. C. Page and Company

(Incorporated)

Publishers

Republished by Gale Research Company, Book Tower, Detroit, 1974

Library of Congress Cataloging in Publication Data

Elson, Louis Charles, 1848-1920.
  The national music of America and its sources.

  Includes bibliographical references.
  1. Music, American. 2. National songs, American
--History and criticism. I. Title.
ML3551.E49   1974   781.7'73   70-159950
ISBN 0-8103-4039-9

PREFACE.

———◆———

IN no department of musical history has there been more of careless and unverified statement, of unquestioning acceptance of tradition, than in the chronicles of our national music. The author by no means claims to have cleared up the mists which hang over some parts of the subject; he may, however, state that where conflicting tales were told, which could neither be confirmed nor disproved, he has presented both sides of the question without prejudice. The origin of "Yankee Doodle," for example, has not been discovered, but it has been pointed out that many things which have been accepted as ascertained facts have by no means the certainty of history.

A slight discursion to show the growth of the national taste in music in America, has been deemed pertinent to the subject. No apology is needed for a full presentation of the music of the Pilgrims and the Puritans, for not only have errors crept into the popular comprehension of this important topic, but this may be regarded as the chief seed whence the early music of our country sprang.

Most of the musical illustrations are drawn from early (often original) editions, in the library of the author.

LOUIS C. ELSON.

CONTENTS.

Contents. vii

CHAPTER VIII.

CHAPTER XI.

LIST OF ILLUSTRATIONS
AND MUSIC.

———

THE
NATIONAL MUSIC OF AMERICA
AND ITS SOURCES.

CHAPTER I.

Introductory — The Seeds of Puritan Music — Synopsis of the Evolution of Congregational Singing — Luther and Calvin —The Music of the Roundheads.

IT is a fallacy to suppose that congregational music (which for a time was the chief music of America) began with Martin Luther. It is true that Luther used it in a degree, and with a power, beyond all of his predecessors in theology, but the inception of congregational music must be credited to the earliest epoch of the Christian Church. Not only was there chorus-singing at the Agapæ, the love-feasts of the Christians of the first century, but the fathers of the Church speak of choral music that must have been very much like the religious music that the Protestants employed centuries later.

The music of the time of the apostles is described chiefly by tradition, but there is so much of verisimilitude in the accounts, and the stories agree so well with each other, that there is at least a strong inference that congregational music existed even in their epoch. Eusebius states that St. Mark taught the first Egyptian converts to chant their prayers together; St. John Chrysostom in his sixth homily declares that the apostles composed the first hymn; Tertullian affirms that the Roman Christians chanted in deep tones; Clemens Romanus (contemporary of St. Paul) states that at the evening meal the Christians generally sang the twenty-third Psalm, and there is evidence that Exodus

XV. and Daniel III. were treated in similar,
choral manner; Origen (in the second century) intimates that the congregations sang
together in his day. But probably the clear-
est statement of early congregational singing
is made by St. John Chrysostom when he
describes part of the Christian service thus :
"The Psalms which we sing united all the
voices in one, and the canticles arise harmo-
niously in unison. Young and old, rich and
poor, women, men, slaves, and citizens, all of
us have formed but one melody together."

The Catholic Church, however, soon abolished the practice of congregational music,
although, in Germany, it still continued, in
spite of the prohibitions of councils and of
popes. The German priests, finding that
they could not prevent their flocks from
joining in the musical part of the services,
wisely resolved to direct this popular singing
in a fitting channel, and numerous simple
songs in praise of the Virgin were composed

especially for this part of musical worship. It was probably from these that the Lutheran chorales first arose.

Some of these old congregational melodies are weirdly intertwined with the history of the time. An example may be cited which not only shows the style of the *Marien-lieder* (as these songs of Mary were called) but the events at times connected with them.

During the fourteenth century the great-est pestilence swept through Europe that has ever been recorded in history. It was called "The Black Death," and claimed its victims by hundreds of thousands, in every country of the old world. In that dreadful epoch men sought to save their lives by isolation. Since a touch, the sweep of a passing garment, might bring death, many barred themselves up in their houses, with such provisions as they could gather, and sustained a strange siege against the invisible enemy without. In such a manner did one of the citizens of Goldberg, in Germany, save his life until a Christmas eve in 1353.[1] He thought himself the last inhabitant of the plague-stricken city, and as the time of the joyous festival approached he could not but recall how many of his old companions had joined with him in merrymaking in the past years; and now he was left alone, in the midst of desolation. The thought must have been borne in upon him that his life was not worth saving at the price of such loneliness, for he unbarred his door and went out into the street to take the plague, if God willed it, and to die. As he went forth he sang the Christmas song that he had sung in the old days with his friends, a " Marien-lied," entitled " Uns ist ein Kindlein heut' geborn." He was astounded to hear a voice respond to his own, and in a

[1] There is some doubt as to the date. Riemann, in his " Deutsche Volkfeste," gives it as 1553, which is probably an error.

little while another citizen had unbarred his door and sang with him; as the two went down the street they were joined by another, and another, until, when they had come to the end of the road at the Niederring, a hill close to the town, there was a little band of twenty-five, men, women, and children, all that was left of the town of Goldberg. Whether it was that the plague had spent its violence, or, which is more probable, that the minds of the survivors were more serene and less afraid of death, none of this little band died of the Black Death. They returned to their homes, set their houses in order, buried their dead, and the town began to prosper anew. But each Christmas eve, for centuries after this event (even to very recent years), the inhabitants of the town gathered together at divine service at midnight, and at two o'clock they marched to the Niederring, where all united in singing the following chorale:

OLD CHORALE.

Uns ist ein Kind-lein Heut ge-born.
To us this day is born a child.

Gott mit uns. Von ei - ner Jung-frau
God with us. His moth-er is a

aus - er-korn. Gott mit uns. Gott mit
vir - gin mild. God with us. God with

uns. Wer will sein wid - er uns?
us. A - gainst us who dare be?

But it was during the epoch of the
Reformation that the seeds were planted
which afterward became the earliest music
of New England. Two diverse influences
were at work within the Protestant lines,
when congregational music had its period of
renascence; on the one hand was Martin

Luther, an ardent musician, who desired to approach the beauty of the Catholic ritual in the music of the Protestant Church; at the other extreme we find John Calvin, a bitter opponent of the fine arts, a man who desired that the music of the Church might attract no attention to itself, but merely become a peg whereon to hang the rhythmic recitation of the psalms.

Luther caused hymn-books with tunes to be published, his earliest collection being the " Enchiridion," printed at Erfurt in 1524. The last remaining copy of this work, preserved in the city library of Strasburg, was destroyed during the German bombardment of that city in the Franco-Prussian war. A Catholic hymnal with tunes, dated seven years earlier than the " Enchiridion " (the first Protestant hymn-book), still exists.

It is a popular error to imagine that the psalms of the Pilgrims were influenced by the music of Luther.   A church choir would have been held in abomination by the early Pilgrims, while Luther believed in alternating choir music with congregational singing. A letter of the great reformer still exists, in which he exhorts a poor parish to make every effort to retain its choir as a musical model for the congregation. We shall see, in a succeeding chapter, how bitter was the Puritan opposition to organ-playing in divine service. This prejudice was entirely Calvinistic, not Lutheran; Luther believed in the employment of the instrument in a very prominent manner. It was in the Lutheran epoch that the custom of interluding upon the organ between each line of the hymn was first introduced. In addition to this display of improvisation the hymn-tune was often given out with a degree of virtuosity that is incredible to the modern musician. To what an extent this organ display was carried by later Protestant churches may be gathered from the accompanying reproduction of one

of the tunes with its "giving out," and in-
terludes as performed in England in the
Protestant churches of the seventeenth
century.

Before dismissing the Lutheran influence
from our consideration, it may be permitted
to give a translation of a poem in praise of
music, which Luther wrote as an introduction
to a little book entitled "Lob und Preis der
loeblichen Kunst Musica. By H. Johann
Walter, Wittenberg, 1538. With a poetical
introduction by Dr. Luther." The poem
seems scarcely known to some of the biog-
raphers of Luther, yet is important as
showing the musical creed of the re-
former.

"DAME MUSICA."

"Of all earth's joys inviting,
  Not one is more delighting
  Than that which lies in singing,
  When tender tones are ringing.
  All guilt and care most quickly flies
  When tones of singing sweetly rise.

And gone is envy, hate and wrong,
And sorrow flies off at the song.
And malice, avarice and greed,
Far from the tones they quickly speed.
And all is well within the heart,
For sin in singing takes no part.
God's blessing rests upon the tune
And for each mortal 'tis a boon,
Since Satan cannot weave his spell
Where tones of Music softly swell.
All people know how David's song
King Saul's existence did prolong;
His harp-tones and rich melody
Caused the king's sorrows swift to fly.
And by sweet music men are stirred
To listen to God's Holy Word.
Eliseus this secret knew
And played the harp with gladness too.
I love the gentle, fragrant Spring,
When all the birds begin to sing.
Then Heaven and Earth have joyous guise
And many melodies arise.
The nightingale with tender trill
With glory all the woods doth fill.
Her song can wondrous joy impart,
And thanks arise in every heart.
But greater thanks to God arise,
Who sent this songster from the skies
To be a model pure and true
To all the souls that music woo.

To sing God's praises she delights
Through all the days and all the nights.
To Him, too, would my song ascend,
That I might praise him without end.

D. MARTIN LUTHER."

In dark contrast with such a noble appreciation of one of God's most glorious gifts, we have the distaste of Calvin for church music, and unfortunately it was the Calvinistic lead that the English Separatists followed, and which moulded the earliest music of New England. The music of the Roundhead in England, and of the Pilgrims in New England, was severe and ascetic. What stronger contrast to such a poem as the above can be imagined than such lines as the following:

" In the black, dismal dungeon of despair,
Pined with tormenting care,
Wracked with my fears,
Drowned in my tears,
With dreadful expectation of my doom
And certain horrid judgment soon to come.

Lord here I lye
Lost to all hope of liberty." [1]

Yet such subjects were not unusual among the pious singers on both sides of the Atlantic. It was fortunate for a good cause that the Roundhead fought much better than he

[1] One could easily form a literary " chamber of horrors " from a host of similar religious poems still existing. Here is a cheerful picture of future punishment:

> " Eternal plagues and heavy chains,
> Tormenting racks and fiery coals,
> And darts t'inflict immortal pains,
> Dipt in the blood of damnèd souls."

About the year 1700, Wigglesworth published a poem (in Boston), on " Babes, Thieves, Heathen, and Heretics," in which he sings thus:

> " They wring their hands, their caitiff hands,
> And gnash their teeth for terror,
> They cry, they roar, for anguish sore,
> And gnaw their tongues for horror.
> But get away without delay;
> Christ pities not your cry:
> Depart to hell, — there you may yell
> And roar eternally."

Nor ought one to forget the more modern hymn:

> " Oh, lovely appearance of Death!
> No sight upon Earth is so fair;
> What glorious pageant of Earth
> Can with a dead body compare? "

It would be an easy task to prove that gloom and religion once walked hand in hand.

sang. He displayed his hatred of the devices of popery by smashing the organs in many of the English churches and cathedrals. Even his war-songs were tinged with a religious swing. One of the favourite songs of the Cromwellian soldiers had a strong flavour of psalm-singing in its measures. It was written by Francis Quarles.[1] Its peculiar character made it easy to burlesque and parody. In the time of the restoration the cavaliers of the court of Charles II. added verses in derision of the Puritans, of which we append an example.

> "What though the king and Parliament
> Do not accord together,
> We have more cause to be content,
> This is our sunshine weather.
>
> .   .   .   .
>
> "A time may come to make us rue
> And time may set us free,
> Except the gallows claim his due
> For hey then, up go we!"

[1] Yet Quarles was a Royalist, and faithful to Charles I. Chappell ("National English Airs"), however, speaks of "Hey then up goe we" as "a great favourite with the Roundhead party."

We also append this song as Cromwell's men used to sing it.

"HEY, THEN, UP WE GO."

A ROUNDHEAD SONG.

Moderate time.

Know then, my breth - ren, Heav'n is

cleare And all the clouds are gone. . .

Firmly.

The righteous now shall flou - rish, And good

days   are   com-ing on; . . . Come then, my

breth - ren, and be glad   And eke re - joyce with

me. . .   Lawne Sleeves and Roch-ets

shall go downe, And hey then up go we. . .

We have now passed in brief review some phases of the inception of that congregational and religious music which was transplanted from Europe to American shores. It soon began to have other phases of development in its new home. Just as in the seventh and eighth centuries, the religious music of France, although born of the Gregorian music of Rome, began to become a school by itself (the "Cantus Gallicanus"), so the music of New England, an offshoot from the Protestant music of the Old World, soon began to go on its own path and present an individuality of its own, while its poetry was taken as a new model by some of the Protestants of England and Scotland.

CHAPTER II.

AMERICAN music was at first planted in a very sterile soil; both Pilgrims and Puritans were opposed to the development of the musical art, yet, by an irony of fate, their psalm-singing became the cradle which cherished the music of America. At the outset we must correct an error which has crept into almost every history of this subject; the Pilgrims were *not* Puritans.[1] Plymouth was settled by Pilgrims, Boston by Puritans.

[1] See "Story of the Pilgrim Fathers," Arber, pp. 246 and 355, and "The Pilgrim Republic," Goodwin, pp. 1–13, 324, etc.

Gradually both sects, in America, approached each other and were finally merged as Congregationalists.

Who, then, were the Pilgrims? All those members of the Separatist Church at Leyden, who voted for the migration to America, whether they were actually able to go there or not, together with such other members as afterward joined their church from England.[1] The Puritans were reformers who claimed to be within the ranks of the Church of England, a free, non-conformist, and greatly dissatisfied kind of Episcopalians; the Separatists, who subsequently became Pilgrims to America, renounced the above church and formed a community by themselves. They were fearfully persecuted, even, at times, by the Puritans. They were sometimes contemptuously called "Brownites" or "Brownists," after Robert Brown, who in 1580 warmly espoused their cause, afterward deserted it,

[1] Arber, p. 355.

but was by no means its founder.[1] The
Separatists received the name of "Pilgrims"
when they left their home in Leyden (where
they had been driven by persecution in England), and sought religious freedom in America. The name appears in a noble sentence
in Bradford's account of the departure:

"So they left that goodly and pleasant city which
had been their resting-place near twelve years; but
they knew they were *Pilgrims*, and looked not much
on those things, but lifted their eyes to the heavens,
their dearest country, and quieted their spirits."

It therefore appears that they applied the
name "Pilgrim" to themselves.

When the Pilgrims came to America, in
1620, their book of Psalmody was a small
volume compiled by the Rev. Henry Ainsworth,[2] one of the Separatist teachers in the
church at Amsterdam. The tune was

[1] Goodwin, p. 13.
[2] "History of Music in New England," by George
Hood, p. 13. The version by Sternhold and Hopkins
was, however, used at Ipswich for a time in the early
colonial days.

printed without any harmony, under some
of the very literal paraphrases of the Psalms.
The poetry often suffered by the exact character of the setting, as the following examples
of the first Psalm may show :

PSALM I. — SCRIPTURAL.

" Blessed is the man that walketh not in the coun-
sel of the ungodly, nor standeth in the way of sinners, nor sitteth in the seat of the scornful."

. . . .

" Therefore the ungodly shall not stand in the
judgment, nor sinners in the congregation of the
righteous."

AINSWORTH.

" O Blessed man that doth not in
The wicked's counsell walk;
Nor stand in sinners' way, nor sit
In seat of scornful folk.

. . . .

" Therefore the wicked shall not in
The Judgment stand upright :
And in th' assembly of the Just
Not any sinfull-wight."

Not all of Ainsworth's selected tunes were
sung by the Pilgrims.   It is said that but

five tunes were familiar. Just what these
five were is not absolutely certain, but they
were probably " Old Hundred," " York,"
" Hackney," " Windsor," and " Martyrs."

The order of service was a very simple one.
In the Separatist congregations in Holland it
had been as follows : Prayer ; Scripture, with
comment ; singing a Psalm ; sermon by the
pastor or by a teacher ; singing another
Psalm ; sacraments on proper Sundays ; a
collection for the poor ; the benediction. It
will be seen that music played no very important part in the proceedings. Winthrop
and his Puritans (including Endicott) soon
gave up their prejudice against " Separatists
and Brownists," and adopted a similar service, but they had even less of music at Boston, the second psalm-singing not taking
place in the service, according to an account
written in 1641.[1]

The "lining-out " of a Psalm (reading each

[1] " Music in America," Ritter, p. 9.

line before singing it) was not used by the
Pilgrim Fathers.   Such a proceeding, most
inartistic from a musical sense, was established by Parliament in England, in 1644.
New England then seems to have taken it
up with avidity.   The result was sometimes
a most awkward one, when the pause neces-
sitated at the end of the line, disturbed, or
even contradicted, the sense of the poem.
Here is an example quoted by Hood in his
" History of Music in New England." [1]

> " The Lord will come, and He will not
> Keep Silence, but speak out."

But as the deacon read the lines they
became rather puzzling :

> " The Lord will come, and he will not."

Which the congregation faithfully repeated.
After which came the rather mystifying request :

> " Keep silence, but speak out."

[1] Page 201.

With the "Bay Psalm-book," this custom of lining-out, sometimes also called "deaconing" the Psalm, began.

"The Bay Psalm-book" (in Boston and vicinity, at least), practically supplanted Ainsworth at once and for ever. The book was the first volume printed in the colonies, although Day, its printer, had issued two unimportant publications before it.[1] The translation was made by various clergymen of the colony (there were about thirty learned ministers here in 1636), but Rev. Thos. Weld, Rev. John Eliot (of Roxbury), and Rev. Richard Mather (of Dorchester) were the chief workers in the field. The faults of two of the poets were summed up in a neat verse by Mr. Shepard, of Cambridge, as follows :

> " You Roxbury poets, keep clear of the crime
> Of missing to give us a very good rhyme.

[1] The first was the " Freeman's Oath " (a " broadside "), the second an almanac for 1639, calculated for New England.

> And you of Dorchester your verses lengthen
> And with the text's own word you will them
>   strengthen."

Mr. Shepard's own fault was evidently that of scorning metre. But the warnings were certainly necessary, for the poetry of the "Bay Psalm-book" was often fearfully and wonderfully made. A few examples may be permitted here.

> " Like as the heart panting doth bray
>   after the water-brooks,
>   even in such wise, O God, my soule
>   after Thee panting looks."   (Ps. xlii, 1.)

> " I as a stranger am become
>   unto my bretherren
>   and am an aliant unto
>   my mother's childerren."   (Ps. lxix, 8.)

> " And sayd He would them waste ; had not
>   Moses stood (whom He chose)
>   'fore Him i'th breach : to turn his wrath
>   lest that He should waste those."
>   (Ps. cvi, 23.)

> " Therefore shall not ungodly men,
>   rise to stande in the doome,
>   nor shall the sinners with the just
>   in their assemblie come."   (Ps. 1, 5).

The dwelling upon the doom of the sinner (as in the last specimen) was always a choice morsel to the *litterateur* of those days.[1] The influence of the " Bay Psalm-book " was enormous. It went through some thirty editions in America, and many in Scotland as well as in England, abundantly proving the final statement of the preceding chapter.

Whatever faults one may find with the poetry of the " Bay Psalm-book," it must be admitted that it was a close and literal translation of the Psalms, in rhyme; it came as near to the old Hebrew version as the English Scriptural version itself. Some of its selections were of great length, the longest being 130 lines. Whatever the length might

---

[1] The damnation of babes who had not been baptised was always a rigid point with both Separatists and Puritans. Here is a verse on the subject by Nathaniel Ward, the pastor of Ipswich. (The Divine Judge speaks):

> " A crime it is ! Therefore in Bliss
> You may not hope to dwell ;
> But unto you I shall allow
> The easiest room in Hell!"

be, the Psalm was sung standing, for Pilgrim
and Puritan stood, rather than knelt, at acts
of greatest devotion.   There was no music
attached to the poems, the traditional old
melodies being employed.   The "Admoni-
tion to the Reader" stated the musical requirements clearly, as follows :

" The verses of these psalmes may be reduced to
six kindes, the first whereof may be sung in very
neere fourty common tunes; as they are collected out
of our chief musicians by Tho. Ravenscroft.

" The second kinde may be sung in three tunes as
Ps. 25, 50 and 67 in our English psalme books.

" The third, may be sung indifferently, as Ps. the
51, 100 and ten commandments, in our English
psalme books, which three tunes aforesaid, comprehend almost all this whole book of psalmes, as being
tunes most familiar to us."

There never was an innovation made in
the Puritan or Pilgrim church, but that a
vehement storm of opposition arose in some
quarters.   This was an outcome of the fundamental principle of the Separatists, that
the elders were the church, that there was

no higher authority but the Divine head, a fine example of religious democracy. The Scriptural injunction, "Tell it unto the church" (Matt. xviii, 17), meant to them that the church was to be a final arbiter, and the phrase, "Let the elders that rule well be counted worthy of double honour" (I. Tim. 16), seemed an incentive to the deacons and elders to assert their individual views whenever they could.

This became a very pretty quarrel. Some believed it right to sing, but thought it wrong to sing the Psalms of David; others believed that Christians should not sing at all, but only praise God with their hearts; some believed it wrong for any but Christians to sing; and others thought that only one should sing, while the assembly should join in silence, and respond Amen.[1]

Boston was of course the first to use the

[1] Hood's "History of Music in New England," pp. 33 *et seq.*

" Bay Psalm-book ; " it was not used in Salem
until 1667.   The following extract from the
Church Records of Plymouth will show how
long and faithfully that organisation had
clung to Ainsworth :

> " May 17th, 1685.   The Elder stayed the church
> after the public worship was ended, and moved to sing
> psalm 130th in another translation, because in Mr.
> Ainsworth's translation, which we sang, the tune was
> so difficult few could follow it — the church readily
> concented thereunto."

In 1692 the Plymouth brethren began to
use the " Bay Psalm-book," as may be seen
from the following extract from their records :

> " Aug. 7th, 1692.   At the conclusion of the Sacra-
> ment the pastor called upon the church to express
> their judgments about this motion ; the vote was
> this : when the tunes are difficult in the translation
> we use, we will sing the psalms now used in our
> neighbor churches in the Bay ; not one brother
> opposed this conclusion.   The Sabbath following,
> Aug. 14th, we began to sing the psalms in course
> according to the vote of the church."

The " in course " of the last sentence

referred to the practice of singing through the psalms in regular order, and then going back to the beginning, as was the custom in Plymouth and in some of the other churches of the Bay.

Up to about this time it was the custom of those who used the "Bay Psalm-book" to write the music in against the verses, but, as they were familiar with but few of the melodies (Ravenscroft's selections were chiefly used), it often happened that only a half-dozen tunes were thus written. Many congregations had only three or four tunes that they could sing passably well. This great defect was overcome about 1690 by printing the music in the psalm-books. The oldest existing music of American imprint is dated 1698, but there is evidence that there were earlier editions. The printing of the Boston edition of 1698 is very poorly done and contains many errors. The tunes given are "Litchfield," "Canterbury" (or "Low Dutch"),

"York," "Windsor," "Cambridge," "St. Davids," "Martyrs," "Hackney" (or "St. Marys," as it was sometimes called),[1] the 100th, 115th, 119th, and 148th psalm-tunes.

Here are a few of the directions printed in the book, for the guidance of the singers.

"Observe how many notes compass the tune is. Next the place of your first note; and how many notes above and below that; so as you may begin the tune of your first note, as the rest may be sung in the compass of your and the people's voices, without squeaking above or grumbling below."

These directions naturally referred to the setting or pitching of the tune, in a day when pitch-pipes and tuning-forks did not exist.

If there had been a quarrel when the "Bay Psalm-book" came in to replace Ainsworth's collection, there was an absolute tempest when singing by note was to replace sing-

[1] Ritter ("Music in America") not only confounds Puritans and Pilgrims, but gives "Hackney" and "St. Marys" as two different tunes, in an important list, (p. 9), a decided and very remarkable error, in this case.

ing by ear. Singing from printed music was soon called "the new way," singing by rote "the old way," and many were the arguments pro and con regarding these two ways.

Here are some of the written objections to the new system :

" 1st, it is a new way — an unknown tongue. 2nd, it is not so melodious as the old way. 3rd, there are so many tunes that nobody can ever learn them. 4th, the new way makes disturbance in churches, grieves good men, exasperates them and causes them to behave disorderly. 5th, it is popish. 6th, it will introduce instruments. 7th, the names of the notes are blasphemous. 8th, it is needless, the old way being good enough. 9th, it requires too much time to learn it. 10th, it makes the young disorderly."

But there were reverend men of culture then existing, who would not give way to the clamour, and Symmes, Thacher, Walter, Dwight, Danforth, Mather, Stoddard, and a host of other divines, arose in favour of the "new way," fighting for musical progress as the Rev. John Cotton had done a century before (1647). A writer in the *New Eng·*

land Chronicle, in 1723, gave his views as follows :[1]

"Truly I have a great jealousy that if we once begin to sing by rule, the next thing will be to pray by rule, and preach by rule ; and then comes popery."

In *The New England Courant* of Sept. 16, 1723 (afterward Benjamin Franklin's paper), we read :

"Last week a Council of Churches, etc., was held in the South part of Braintree to regulate the disorders occasioned by regular singing at that place."

Before this time there had been great reverence for all psalm-singing in every part of the colony, as is proved by the doffing of caps when any psalm-tune was sung anywhere, and by the fact that in Plymouth, in 1660, "Robert Bartlett having spoken contemptuously of the ordinance of psalm-singing, was censured by the General Court."

The "old way" must have been the acme of all that was inartistic, judging by the

[1] Quoted by Brooks, " Olden-time Music," p. 20.

accounts that are left of it. Rev. Dr. Walter[1] said of it that it "sounded like five hundred different tunes roared out at the same time." So little attention was paid to time that the singers were often two words apart, "producing noises," continues Mr. Walter, "so hideous and disorderly, as is bad beyond expression."

To turn again to the defenders of the "old way;" here are a few of the "questions of conscience" which they put to their opponents:[2]

"Whether you do believe that singing in the worship of God ought to be done skilfully?

"Whether you do believe that skillfulness in singing may ordinarily be gained in the use of outward means, by the blessing of God?

[1] Rev. Thomas Walter, of Roxbury, Mass., who so heartily defied the adherents of the "old way," that, in 1721, he brought out "The Grounds and Rules of Musick Explained" — the first practical American book of musical instruction.

[2] Quoted from a tract, entitled, "Cases of Conscience about Singing Psalms, Briefly Considered and Resolved." 1723.

"Whether they who purposely sing a tune different from that which is appointed by the pastor or
elder to be sung, are not guilty of acting disorderly,
and of taking God's name in vain also, by disturbing
the order of the Sanctuary?"

As late as Aug. 21, 1771, John Adams
bears witness to the continued existence of
the two schools of song, by writing in his
Diary:

"Went to meeting at the old Presbyterian Society; the Psalmody is an exact contrast to that of
Hartford.   It is in the *old way* as we call it, — all
the drawling, quavering discord in the world."

The battle began with the opening of the
eighteenth century.   But, if there were evi-
dences of musical barbarism in New England at this time, there were also decided
proofs of musical progress.

A work published in London, in 1673,
entitled: "Observations Made by the Curious in New England," informs us that "in
Boston there are no musicians by trade.   A
dancing-school was set up but put down; a

fencing-school is allowed." But in 1717 we find a singing society begun in Boston, "to practice singing by note."

In 1712 the Rev. John Tufts, of New-bury, brought out a collection of psalm-tunes; about two years later he followed it with a second volume. The ice was broken, and from this time on there followed a succession of sacred collections in sufficient profusion to prove that New England was musical in at least one direction.

The next step forward was the establish-ment of choirs. We have seen, in the pre-ceding chapter, that Martin Luther believed in a combination of choir and congregational singing; the Congregationalists of New Eng-land (for the name was now applied to the churches of the colony) came to this result about 250 years later than the German re-former. The strife between the adherents and opponents of the "new way" had led to a revolution in music; a lesser revolution now took place against the habit of "dea-coning" or "lining-out" the psalms and hymns. Doctor Watts's Psalms [1] were used in the colony from 1741, when the first New England edition was printed. In the preface of this work the author rebukes the custom of "lining-out" thus:

> "It were to be wished that all congregations and private families would sing as they do in foreign Protestant countries, without reading line by line. Though the author has done what he could to make the sense complete in every line or two; yet many inconveniences will always attend this unhappy manner of singing."

In some churches the clergyman was able to put aside the custom without any ado, but in many cases the elders, deacons, and general congregation indulged in their customary squabble over the matter, and there were

---

[1] An edition of Watts's Hymns was printed by Doctor Franklin in Philadelphia in the same year that the New England (Boston) edition of Watts's Psalms was issued,— 1741.

plenty of combatants on the side of "the good old way."

The beginning of choirs was less tumultuous, because more gradual. The singing-schools (for many others followed the one which Boston established in 1717) were an important factor in the advance, for the congregations were no longer on the same level of musical ability, or rather weakness ; the members who were skilled in music were apt to gather together, without any express command from the minister, and without being assigned to any especial position in the meeting-house. Choirs had therefore crept into some churches before 1750, although there is no official record of the fact. When official recognition was given, the custom had become so habitual that no earnest remonstrance was made, even by the chronic obstructionists.

Here are a few of the earliest edicts regarding New England church choirs :

"1762. The parish voted that those who had learned the art of singing may have liberty to sit in the front gallery. *They did not take the liberty.*

"1780. The parish requested Jonathan Chaplin, Jr., and Lieutenant Spafford to assist Deacon Daniel Spafford in raising the tune in the Meeting house.

"1785. The parish desire the singers, both male and female, to sit in the gallery, and will allow them to sing once upon each Lord's day *without reading by the deacon.*" ("History of Rowley," p. 93.)

The last sentence explains why the singers rejected the first proposal; they were evidently opposed to the "lining-out" system.

"1773. The seats for the choir were designated by the First Parish in Ipswich, being two back on each side of the front alley." ("History of Ipswich.")

A similar provision was made at the Hamlet (now called Hamilton, Mass.) in 1764, in Chebacco in 1788,[1] and the custom was soon imitated by many other parishes. Worcester came into line in 1770–1773. A final combat on the "lining-out" question took place here

[1] Felt's "History of Ipswich."

in 1779, on the first Sunday that the choir displayed its abilities.

"After the hymn had been read by the minister, the aged and venerable Deacon Chamberlain, unwilling to desert the custom of his fathers, rose and read the first line according to the usual practice. The singers, prepared to carry the alteration into effect, proceeded without pausing at the conclusion. The white-haired officer of the church with the full power of his voice read on, until the louder notes of the collected body overpowered the attempt to resist the progress of improvement, and the deacon, deeply mortified at the triumph of musical reformation, seized his hat and retired from the Meeting house in tears." ("History of Worcester.")

In the last half of the eighteenth century, because of the victory of the choirs and singing-schools, books of music began to follow each other with great profusion. Newburyport, Northampton, Worcester, and Boston, all sent forth their various musical collections. "The American Harmony," "The Gentleman and Ladies Musical Companion," "The Psalm-singer's Amusement,"

"The Massachusetts Harmony," "The Suf-
folk Harmony," and "Laus Deo," all followed in quick succession,[1] the last named
being especially interesting, from the fact
that it was the first book printed from
music type in this country, all its predecessors being engraved works.   Naturally,
with such a musical activity going on

[1] In order that the list of eighteenth century music-books
may be reasonably complete, we append the following table
of dates and titles : Rev. John Tufts's " Easy introduction
to the Art of Singing Psalm tunes," Newbury, 1712 (?);
" An Introduction to the singing of Psalm tunes," by the
same author, Boston, 1714; " Psalterium Americanum,"
Dr. Cotton Mather, 1718; " Grounds and Rules of Musick
explained," Dr. Thomas Walter, 1721; " Watts' Psalms,"
Boston, 1741 ; " Tate and Brady's Psalms," 1741 (?); " Bar-
nard's Psalms," Boston, 1752; Prince's revision of the
" Bay Psalm-book," 1758; "A Collection of the best
Psalm tunes," Josiah Flagg, Boston, 1764 (engraved by
Paul Revere; the largest collection up to this time in
New England, and, for the first time, we find light music
intermingled with the psalm-tunes) ; " Grounds and Rules
of Music," Bayley, Newburyport, 1764; "The New England Psalm-singer, or American Chorister," Billings, Boston, 1770; after these (between 1770 and 1800) there
appeared nearly forty different volumes devoted to music,
almost invariably of the sacred order.

throughout New England, there was also some agitation regarding instrumental music. A few bold spirits desired to introduce the organ into the divine service here, as it was used in foreign countries ; but in this matter the victory was gained with the greatest difficulty, and the conflict of opinions lasted a full century.

As early as 1713, Mr. Brattle, a Puritan of Boston, but a man of artistic instincts, and much more liberal than his fellow citizens in theological matters, gave, by will, an organ to the Brattle Square Church, with the condition that the offer should be accepted within a year after his decease, and they should "procure a sober person to play skilfully thereon with a loud noise." The sly quotation from the Scripture shows that Mr. Brattle felt that the pill needed some sugar-coating, and his doubts upon the subject are further illustrated by a proviso, by which, if his church declined the proffered gift, it was

to be offered to King's Chapel,[1] the representative of the Church of England in Boston
at that time. The vote of the Puritan church
was overwhelmingly against the innovation,
and the sentence, " We do not think it
proper to use the same in the public worship
of God," is terse and to the point. The
organ was therefore given to King's Chapel,
which used it until 1756, when a new
and larger one was bought. An organist
was imported from London to play upon
the instrument. This was the first pipe-
organ set up in a New England church, and
its coming caused about as much commotion
as the entrance of the wooden horse into
Troy ; Cotton Mather, who believed in congregational singing, and had helped the

[1] The edifice still stands at the corner of School and
Tremont Streets, and the old organ is also still in exist-
ence; the instrument was sold, in 1756, to St. Paul's
Church, Newburyport, which, in 1836, sold it to St.
John's Church in Portsmouth, where it is said to be in
reasonably good condition even now.

musical cause with an excellent translation of the Psalms for vocal purposes, burst forth in fierce diatribes when the organ was inaugurated, and denounced the wickedness of Boston roundly, in his Thursday lecture.[1]

There is inferential proof that the Puritans did not bother themselves with instrumental music of any kind. Henry M. Brooks, in his " Olden-Time Music," says (p. 33) :

" An examination of the earliest ' inventories ' in the Probate Office of Essex County fails to find record of any musical instruments appraised in the estates settled therein. While every pot, skillet, gridiron, article of wearing-apparel, old chair and table, bed, bolster, and pillow, silver spoon, pewter dish, bushel of corn, indeed articles of the most trifling nature, are carefully enumerated, no lutes,

[1] The weekly "lectures" in Boston were of the nature of prayer-meetings, and the address was not at all different from what we to-day would call a sermon. As regards the singing of psalms, Cotton Mather thus expresses himself: "The singing of psalms is a supplicating of God himself, wherein by humble prayer we beg the pardon of our sins." Dr. Cotton Mather was the most voluminous writer in the colonies, his publications amounting to three hundred and eighty-two works!

citterns, spinets, harpsichords, flutes or viols are
mentioned. This would seem to show that the early
settlers did not possess these instruments, or that at
least they must have been rarely seen here."

Although we have called the organ described above the earliest of New England,
there evidently was a more primitive instrument in existence in Boston, in Mr. Brattle's
house, in 1711, for in the Diary of the Rev.
Joseph Green, published by the Essex Institute (collection of 1869, May), we read,
under date of May 29, 1711 : " I was at Mr.
Thomas Brattle's ; heard ye organs." But
the information is very vague.[1]

[1] Mr. Brattle seems to have been a man of more than
ordinary culture, certainly far in advance of his surroundings. It would be delightful to ascertain what kind of an
organ he had at his house, but the Rev. Doctor Green is
tantalisingly brief in all his notes. He visited Boston in
May, 1711, as the following note indicates :

" May 28th. I went to Boston with my daughter Ann ;
log'd at Brother Gerrish."

This is immediately followed by the important note:

" May 29th. I was at Thomas Brattle's, heard ye
organs and saw strange things in a microscope."

Samuel Sewall also mentions " Mr. Brattle's organs "
in his diary, Sept. 3, 1708 (Vol. II., p. 235).

The second organ of New England was set up at Newport (Trinity Church), in 1733.

It is curious to find a young Bostonian, a Harvard graduate, Edward Bromfield, Jr., building an organ, unaided, in 1745, but as the talented young man died the next year, at twenty-three years of age, he was unable to complete his instrument (he intended it to have twelve hundred pipes), and we find no record of its being set up or used in any church.

In 1770, for the first time in American history, a Congregational church allowed an organ to be used in its service, but this happened in Providence, where bigoted lines were never very strongly drawn.

The chronology of the early New England church organs would seem to be about as follows: King's Chapel, Boston, the first; Trinity Church, Newport, the second; Trinity Church, Boston, the third; Christ Church, Boston, the fourth, and St. Peter's

Church, Salem, the fifth, none of these being Congregational or Puritan churches.

In 1790 the Brattle Square Church, which had declined the offer of the first church organ of New England, changed its mind regarding the wickedness of the matter, and ordered an organ built in London, probably the second used in a Congregational church in New England.[1] It will serve to show how slowly the prejudice against the instrument was dying out, when it is stated that one of its leading members offered to pay back to the church all its outlay, and even to give a sum to the poor of Boston, if they would allow him to cause the unhallowed instrument to be thrown into Boston Harbour!

Nor was this prejudice confined to America only; in Scotland it is even to-day not entirely

---

[1] A German musician, named Hans Gram, was the organist. He was looked upon as one of the leading musicians of the country at that time. A few years later a better foreign musician came to Boston, — Gottlieb Graupner, of whom we shall speak in a later chapter.

eradicated; in Boston, a century ago, one of the Congregational churches appealed to its London benefactor, the wealthy Mr. Hollis, for assistance in establishing an organ in their meeting-house. He promptly responded by sending them five hundred copies of a tract, entitled "The Christian religion shines brightest in its own dress, and to paint it is but to deform it."

The bass viol (violoncello) was accepted in some Congregational churches long before the organ was tolerated.

CHAPTER III.

In 1798 the following advertisement appeared in the *Columbian Centinel* (Boston):

"Just published, price 1 dollar, neatly bound and lettered, sold by E. Larkin, No. 47 Cornhill, ' The Columbian Songster,' and Free Mason's ' Pocket Companion.' A collection of the newest and most celebrated Sentimental, Convivial, Humorous, Satirical, Pastoral, Hunting, Sea, and Masonic Songs, being the largest and best collection ever published in America. Selected by S. Larkin."

The above is a proof that music had left the circumscribed limits of psalm singing in Boston. A similar collection (in possession of the author) is entitled "The American Musical Miscellany," and was published in

60

the same year in Northampton, Mass. In
the preface of the latter work the following
sentence occurs :

" A general preference has been given to American productions, and perhaps nothing will more
effectually exhibit the progress of the human mind in
the refinements which characterize the age, than the
songs, which from general consent, are now in vogue."

That this boasting preamble was not carried
out in the American musical numbers of that
time may readily be seen from the following
composition, which is by no means poorer than
other American compositions in the book.

Concerts of secular music had also now
begun. As early as 1756, a public-spirited
citizen, named Stephen Deblois, built a
" Concert Hall " in Boston,[1] and many enter-

[1] This stood on the southern corner of Hanover and
Court Streets. This was at that time the fashionable end
of the town. Washington Street was at that time called
Marlboro Street, its northern extremity was called Cornhill, its extreme southern end, on "the neck," was the
only part then called Washington Street. North Street,
Cornhill, India Street, and Broad Street were fashionable
thoroughfares, the last-named containing the finest shops.

ODE to COLUMBIA's FAVOURITE SON.

Sung by the INDEPENDENT MUSICAL SOCIETY, on the arrival of THE PRESIDENT
at the TRIUMPHAL ARCH, in BOSTON, October 24, 1789.

SOLO.——*The Bass to this part to be sung very softly by one voice.*

Great Washington, the Hero's come, Each heart exulting hears the sound ; See!

thousands their deliv'.-rer throng, And shout him wel-come all a-round.

Chorus.
[To be sung briskly.]

Now in full chorus burst the song, And shout the deeds of Washington!

tainments were given there. Other concerts took place frequently in Brattle Street, where a " Music Hall " existed.

In the early concerts music was combined with dancing, for not only were there occasional fancy dances given in the programme, but the concert was frequently followed by a ball, both entertainments being given at a single admission. The following from the *Boston Chronicle* of November 1, 1768, speaks for itself :

> " *This is to acquaint the Gentlemen and Ladies*
> *that a*
> CONCERT of MUSIC
> *will be performed*
> On Monday, the 21st inst., at Six o'Clock in the Evening, at the Music Hall in Brattle-Street, opposite Dr. Cooper's Meeting-House. After the concert is over, the Gentlemen and Ladies may have a Ball till Eleven o'clock."

The tickets were one shilling and sixpence sterling, not an exorbitant price. We are sorry to see the connection between music and dancing carried so far that the organist

of Trinity Church, in 1774, advertises that
he is about to open a *dancing - school* in
addition to his musical duties.

There were earlier secular concerts than
the one mentioned above. The earliest of
which we have any record was given in
Faneuil Hall, Boston, in 1744, for the benefit of the poor, while, less than a score of
years later, Mr. Dipper,[1] organist of King's
Chapel, was constantly giving musical entertainments and exhibitions. The tickets to
these concerts were generally half a dollar
each.

The programmes were sometimes of a
very heterogeneous description, as witness
the following one, given in Salem, May 15,
1798 :[2]

PART IST.

Grand Symphony.   By Pleyl
Song : On by the spur of valour goaded, Mr.
        Collins.   Shield

        [1] Hawthorne alludes to this musician in "Twice-told
Tales."
        [2] Quoted by Brooks, "Olden-Time Music," p. 167.

Clarinet Quartetto, Messrs. Granger, Lau-
mont, von Hagen and Graupner.   Vogel
Song: He pipes so sweet, Mrs. Graupner.   Hook
Concerto on the French Horn, Mr. Rosier.   Ponton
A favorite new song: Little Sally's wooden
ware, Miss Solomon.   Arnold
Full Piece.   Hayden

PART 2ND.

Quartetto: Who shall deserve the glowing
Praise, Mrs. Graupner, Mr. Granger,
Mr. Collins, and Mr. Mallet.   Linly
Concerto on the Clarinet composed and per-
formed by Mr. Shaffer.
A new favorite echo Song: How do you
Do? Mrs. Graupner and accompanied
on the Hautboy by Mr. Graupner.   Hook
Concerto on the Violin, Laumont.   Foder
A comic Irish Song: Boston News, Mr.
Collins.
Concerto on the Hautboy, the composition
of the celebrated Fisher, Mr. Graupner.
Duet, Hey Dance to the Fiddle and Tabor,
from the much admired Opera of Lock
and Key, Mrs. Graupner and Mr.
Collins.
Finale.   Pleyl

Number of performers, 12. Doors to be opened
at 6 o'clock and the performance to begin precisely

at half after seven.   In consequence of the advice of
some friends, Mr. Graupner has reduced the price
of the Tickets to half a Dollar each."

It must not be supposed that such an
olla podrida of music was below the aver-
age of the epoch ; on the contrary, the above
concert was given by the best musician of
America, up to that time.[1]   The most prominent musician before Graupner's time (we
shall hear more of Graupner in a later
chapter) was Josiah Flagg.   Mr. Flagg compiled and published, in 1764, the largest
musical collection that had ever been printed
in New England ; but he did more than this,
in 1773 he established a band, became its
leader, and gave many concerts in Faneuil
Hall, and elsewhere, on one occasion direct-
ing fifty musicians.[2]

The American composer now enters upon

[1] Beethoven's fifth symphony was performed in Boston
less than seventy years ago, divided into *three sections*, with
lighter music interspersed, for fear that the audience
would grow weary !

[2] Ritter's " Music in America," p. 44.

the scene. It will readily be understood,
however, that from such seeds as we have
described no very bountiful harvest of native
compositions could result. The first attempts
were rather puerile. The first composer of
even local reputation was William Billings.

In 1770 the first book of native composition appeared in the musical field. It was
entitled "The New England Psalm-singer :
or American Chorister. Containing a number of Psalm-tunes, Anthems, and Canons.
In four and five parts. (Never before published.) Composed by William Billings, a
Native of Boston, in New England. Math.
XXI, 16. 'Out of the Mouth of Babes
and Sucklings hast Thou perfected Praise.'
James V, 13. 'Is any merry? Let him
sing Psalms.'

> "' O, Praise the Lord with one consent,
> And in this grand design,
> Let Britain and the Colonies
> Unanimously join.'

Boston, New England.   Printed by Edes &
Gill.''

It has become quite the fashion to point
shafts of sarcasm at Billings, and it must
be confessed that some of his music builds
a wofully ambitious edifice out of very slen-
der material; yet occasionally one finds a
peculiar strength in some of the expressions
of his muse, and he may well be called a
musical John Bunyan.   There is a certain
vigour in :

> " Let tyrants shake their iron rod,
>   And Slavery clank her galling chains;
> We'll fear them not, we'll trust in God;
>   New England's God forever reigns.''

The man himself was an eccentric and
uncouth character, easily ridiculed, even in
his own days.   He was born in Boston,
October 7, 1746, and died there, September
29, 1800.   He was a tanner, and is said to
have chalked down his earliest compositions
upon sides of leather.   His musical educa-

tion was probably limited to the singing-school, but this in nowise dismayed him, for he believed (as Schumann did in his early days) that natural taste would guide the true musician in composition, without the necessity of studying any rules ; indeed, he states this fact in the preface of his book, as follows :

" To all Musical Practitioners.

" Perhaps it may be expected by some, that I should say something concerning Rules for Composition; to these I answer that *Nature is the best dictator*, for all the hard dry studied rules that ever were prescribed, will not enable any person to form an Air. . . . It must be Nature, Nature must lay the foundation, Nature must inspire the thought. . . . For my own part, as I don't think myself confined to any rules of Composition laid down by any that went before me, neither should I think (were I to pretend to lay down rules) that any who come after me were any ways obligated to adhere to them, any further than they should think proper. So in fact I think it is best for every Composer to be his own Carver."

Governor Samuel Adams and Doctor Pierce, of Brookline, took great interest in the enthusiastic choir singer and composer. The latter said of him, that when they sang side by side, he (Rev. Dr. Pierce) could not hear his own voice, which was no still, small voice, either.[1]

Billings was deformed in person, blind in one eye, one leg shorter than the other, untidy in dress and person, and a tremendous snuff-taker, carrying his tobacco around with him in his coat, the pocket of which was purposely made of leather.   Many loved to play practical jokes upon him, even while his music was accepted with enthusiasm on every hand (possibly because it always had a spice of patriotism in it, a much prized quality at the time of the Revolution), and we read of some playful boys tying a couple of cats by the tails to the sign over his music store in Boston ; one can imagine his feelings at coming out and finding the caterwauling animals suspended under the proud legend, "Billings' Music."

[1] Gould, "History of Church Music in America," p. 46.

His glowing enthusiasm for his art was probably unfeigned ; his earnest prefaces bear the mark of sincerity, and, judging by the preface to his next collection, published eight years after the one described above, he began to discard his " Babe and Suckling " and " Natural composition " theories, for he says :[1]

" . . . About ten years ago I published a book entitled ' The New England Psalm-singer ' and truly a most masterly performance I then thought it to be. How lavish was I of encomium on this my infant production. . . . But to my great mortification . . . I have discovered that many pieces were never worth my printing or your inspection."

We have already intimated that the patriotic side of Billings was the favourite one with his public ; he was always at fever-heat, nor did he consider it at all unfitting to drag in paraphrases of the Scriptures in dealing with Revolutionary topics.[2] His " Lamentation over Boston " boldly appropriated the beauti-

[1] Preface to the " Singing Master's Assistant."
[2] Gould, " History of Church Music in America."

ful 137th Psalm to weep over the fact that
Boston was in British hands.   He begins :

" By the Rivers of *Watertown* we sat down; yea,
we wept when we remembered Boston."

He continues in the same strain :

" If I forget thee, O Boston, —
.   .   .   .   .   .
Then let my numbers cease to flow,
Then be my Muse unkind;
Then let my tongue forget to move,
And ever be confined.
Let horrid jargon split the air,
And rive my nerves asunder;
Let hateful Discord grate my ear,
As terrible as Thunder."

Poor Billings, however, yielded to the
demon of "fugueing" in several of his compositions, such fugueing as might make
Bach's bones rattle.   Indeed, he says :

" There is more variety in one piece of fugueing
music than twenty of plain song.   For while the
tones do most sweetly coincide and agree, the words
are seemingly engaged in a musical warfare; and
excuse the paradox, if I further add, that each part
seems determined, by dint of harmony and strength

of accent, to drown his competitor in an ocean of harmony."

Holyoke, one of Billings's more cultivated successors, held a very different opinion in this matter, for he says that this sort of music " produces a trifling effect."[1]

" For the parts falling in, one after another, each conveying a different idea, confound the sense, and render the music a mere jargon of words."

There need, however, be no discussion about the *fugues* used by the early American composers, for they were not fugues at all, merely short passages of contrapuntal imitation, generally defying counterpoint in a manner that proved that freedom was a fundamental principle with every musical American. Not one of the composers aforesaid had the remotest idea of what constituted a fugue, although they glibly explained "fugueing" in almost all of their musical collections.

[1] Preface to " Harmonia Americana." Boston, 1791.

That Billings remained poor in spite of his popularity, may be proved by the following appeal, following an advertisement of the publication of one of his works by subscription, (possibly the " Continental Harmony "). The notice is taken from the *Massachusetts Magazine* of August, 1792.

" *Address to the Benevolent of every Denomination.*   The distressed situation of Mr. Billings' family has so sensibly operated on the minds of the committee as to induce their assistance in the intended publication."

Billings is said to have been the first to introduce the violoncello in New England churches, a great step toward the eventual introduction of the organ.   He was also probably the earliest to introduce the pitch-pipe to " set the tune."

From all the accounts of Billings we believe him to have been a great music-lover, an enthusiast, honest in his convictions, but uncouth in expression and utterly untrained in the school of music which he undertook to compose, the most dignified and difficult school of any.

Yet we are not of those who despise his "woodnotes wild," nor are we disposed to jest at his honest love of an art of which he stood only upon the threshold. He was the right man in the right place. A good composer in the higher forms would have utterly failed to appeal to the American public of that time. William Billings broke the ice which was congealing New England's music, and America owes him a great debt of gratitude spite of his few thousand errors of harmony.

After him there came a long procession of similar composers. Andrew Law was of higher education and had more practical knowledge; Jacob Kimball deserted legal study for music, was less original than Billings, and died in the poorhouse; Samuel Holyoke opposed the fugue tunes; Daniel

Read, Timothy Swan, and Jacob French also deserve mention.

Oliver Holden has a little stronger claim upon our attention, for he composed " Coronation," which serves to perpetuate his name. He was a carpenter by trade, a resident of Charlestown, Mass. He left his saws and planes to become a music teacher. He published and edited five volumes of music. He was among the first to use music type in Boston. We give a reproduction of " Coronation " the way it appeared in its first edition,[1] which may also serve to show the style of musical typography in its earliest New England stages.

We have now reached the time when music had a local habitation and a name in Massachusetts and throughout New England. Music teachers had settled in Boston. The

[1] From the " Union Harmony, or Universal Collection of Sacred Music: printed Typographically, at Boston, by Isaiah Thomas and Ebenezer T. Andrews, 1793."

Coronation. C. M. Words by the Rev. Mr. Medley. pia. Original.

All hail the power of Je-sus' name, Let angels prostrate fall, Bring forth the royal di-a-dem, And crown him Lord of all, Bring forth the royal di-a-dem, and crown him Lord of all.

price of a music lesson, as gleaned from the old advertisements, was from half a dollar to seventy-five cents, the more eminent teachers contenting themselves with the latter price. The teacher was generally obliged to lend his piano to the pupil for practising purposes (many advertisements offer this advantage), since the instrument was a great rarity at even the beginning of the nineteenth century, in Boston. The pupils played pieces by Gyrowetz and sometimes even attempted Haydn, but far more generally it was "Washington's March" or some "Battle-piece"[1] that struck wonder into the hearts of the auditors. The change in manners may be thoroughly shown by the following quotation

---

[1] The "Battle of Prague" was by no means the earliest of these warlike compositions; the author possesses a "Sonata pour le Clavecin ou Forte-piano, qui represente La Bataille de Rosbach" [fought Nov. 5, 1757, between Frederic the Great, and the French] "Composées par Mr. Bach." Evidently by J. Christian Bach, son of the great master.

from a letter written by Brissot de Warville,[1] from Boston, in 1788 :

"You no longer meet here that Presbyterian austerity which interdicted all pleasures, even that of walking, which forbade travelling on Sunday, which persecuted men whose opinions were different from their own. The Bostonians unite simplicity of morals with that French politeness and delicacy of manners which render virtue more amiable. They are hospitable to strangers and obliging to friends; they are tender husbands, fond and almost idolatrous parents, and kind masters. Music, which their teachers formerly proscribed as a diabolical art, begins to make part of their education. In some houses you hear the forte-piano. This art it is true is still in its infancy; but the young novices who exercise it are so gentle, so complaisant, and so modest, that the proud perfection of art gives no pleasure equal to what they afford."

[1] Jean Pierre Brissot, who assumed the name "De Warville," was a celebrated Girondist. He was born at Chartres, 1754. He became a prominent lawyer in Paris and wrote some important legal works. He was also a pamphleteer and journalist. His coming to America was in the interests of an abolition society which he founded in Paris, called "The Friends of the Blacks." He entered heart and soul into the spirit of our Revolution. Returning to France, he was tried with the Girondists (see account of the "Marseillaise" in the next chapter) and died on the guillotine, with bravery and dignity, Oct. 31, 1793.

CHAPTER IV.

European National Songs — The Voice of Freedom in For-
eign Countries — " Lilliburlero " — Scottish War-songs
— Koerner's " Song of the Sword " — The Music of the
Reign of Terror; " Ça Ira " and " La Carmagnole " —
The " Marseillaise " —The English National Anthem
and Its American Uses — " My Country, 'tis of Thee."

ALTHOUGH this chapter may seem to be
a digression from the strict line of our subject, since it speaks chiefly of foreign national
music, the student of history will find a kin-
ship among the songs of Freedom in every
clime, and some of the tunes cited will be
found to have exerted a direct influence upon
American music. It has been well said —
" Happy are those nations which have no
history," for history is too often only the
record of the strife, injustice, and oppression
of mankind. Out of these evils beautiful
music is born. Shelley's lines,

" Most wretched men,
Are cradled into poetry by Wrong;
They learn in suffering what they teach in Song,"

can be justly applied to much national music. Schubert once complained that the public seemed to love those songs best which he had written in the greatest agony ; the same is often true of national music ; the groans of the oppressed become a stirring art-work, and Music is the child of Sorrow, national or individual.

It sometimes occurs, also, that a trivial song becomes the pivot upon which the greatest events may swing. Probably the most remarkable instance of this is found in the English Revolution of 1688, when " Lilliburlero " exerted an influence out of all proportion to its jovial music and its frivolous words.[1]

[1] Hosts of authors have alluded to " Lilliburlero," in fiction. Sterne speaks of it in " Tristram Shandy," Thackeray in " Henry Esmond," Robert Louis Stevenson in " Treasure Island," etc.

To understand the full meaning of this production it is necessary to comprehend the stern bigotry of Richard Talbot, whom it satirised.   Talbot had been a firm royalist during the time of the Commonwealth, and had even returned to England from Holland (whither he had fled after the defeat of the king's forces), with the avowed determination of avenging the decapitation of Charles I. by the assassination of Cromwell.   He was a man of undaunted courage and did not propose to strike in the dark ; he therefore wrote a pamphlet, which he entitled " Killing no Murder," and sent it to the Protector. Cromwell is said never to have smiled again after reading the threatening essay.   But Cromwell's own secret service was phenomenally effective, and he had loyal friends enough to prevent the murder being accomplished.   Talbot therefore returned to the Continent, a disappointed man.

At the time of the Restoration it was very

natural to find Richard Talbot in England
again, and now on the top wave of prosperity. He was made Earl of Tyrconnel,
and afterward still further promoted by
James II. Ireland had been in a most
discontented state during the English con-
vulsions. In 1641 a rebellion took place,
which was accompanied by more than one
massacre of Protestants. At one of these
the rallying cry of the Irish, by which they
might recognise each other in the tumult,
is said to have been " Lilliburlero " and
" Bullen al-a," which gives the only clue to
the strange title of the song. In 1687 Talbot had been lieutenant-general in Ireland,
and had distinguished himself by the arbi-
trary way in which he had treated the Protestants. In October, 1688, James II. made
him his full deputy-lieutenant with greater
powers than ever before.

All England, and the Protestant part of
Ireland, was in a ferment at the injustice

of the appointment. Thomas, Lord Wharton (1640–1715), a prominent Whig, took the occasion to write a set of jingly verses about the matter, which he entitled "Lilliburlero." He fitted his rhymes to a pretty quickstep, written by Henry Purcell (the greatest of English composers), in 1678. It is impossible to exaggerate the effect of the song. Bishop Burnet says:

"A foolish ballad was made at that time, treating the Papists, and chiefly the Irish, in a very ridiculous manner, which had a burden, said to be Irish words, 'Lero, lero, lilliburlero,' that made an impression on the army that cannot be imagined by those who saw it not. The whole army, and at last the people, both in city and country, were singing it perpetually. And perhaps never had so slight a thing so great an effect."

Lord Wharton, after the change of dynasty, made the boast that he had rhymed James out of three kingdoms, but he does not take account of the fact that the music played a most important part in the popu-

larity of the song. In fact, in this case,
a musical composer may be credited with
being one of the chief factors in a great
revolution. The words ran as follows:

> " Ho! broder Teague,[1] dost hear de decree?
>   Lilliburlero, bullen a-la.
> Dat we shall have a new deputie,
>   Lilliburlero, bullen a-la.

> " Ho! by Saint Tyburn, it is de Talbote,
> And he shall cut all de Englishmen's troate.
>   (Refrain.)

> " Dough by my soul de English do praat
> De law's on dare side, and Creish knows what.
>   (Refrain.)

> " But if dispence do come from de pope,
> We'll hang Magna Charta and dem in a rope.

> " For de good Talbote is made a lord,
> And wid brave lads is coming aboard.

> " Who all in France have taken a sware,
> Dat dey will have no Protestant heir.

[1] " Brother Teague " was then the nickname of the
Irishman as " John Bull " is of the Englishman at present.
The dialect of the song is absurdly un-Irish.

" Ara ! but why does he stay behind ?
Ho ! by my soul, 'tis a Protestant wind.

" But see de Tyrconnel is now come ashore
And we shall have commissions galore.

" An he dat will not go to de Mass
Shall be turn out, an look like an ass.

" Now, now de hereticks all shall go down
By Chrish and St. Patrick de nation's our own.

" Dere was an old prophecy found in a bog,
' Ireland shall be ruled by an ass and a dog.'

" And now dis prophecy is come to pass
For Talbote's de dog [1] and James is de ass."

More trivial words were never written, but
the pretty music sugar-coated the pill, and
" Lilliburlero " entered the list of great revolutionary songs.   We append the quickstep
of Purcell.

If James II. gave rise to this historical
song, his son gave rise to better music,
and his grandson to infinitely finer ballads.

---

[1] A pun is here intended, for a " Talbot " is a large
hunting hound.

" LILLIBURLERO."

Hey, Broth-er Teague, dost hear de decree,

Lil - li - bur - ler - o, bul - len - a - la;

Dat we shall have a new dep - u - tee?

Lil - li - bur - ler - o, bul - len - a - la.

Le - ro, le - ro, lil - li - bur - ler - o,

Lil - li - bur - ler - o, bul - len - a - la. ·

Le - ro, le - ro, lil - li - bur - ler - o,

Lil - li - bur - ler - o, bul - len - a - la.

The Scottish Jacobite songs illustrate every phase of a hopeless struggle.　The weak attempt of the man who might have been James III. (the " Old Pretender " or the " Old Chevalier " — of St. George — as his opponents and adherents respectively called him) to regain his throne, led to the employment of the very ancient tune, now known as " Scots wha hae," as a war-song, and also to "What's a' the Steer, Kimmer?" while the music which crystallised around the more courageous efforts of his son, Charles Edward (the " Young Pretender," the "Young Chevalier," or — best of all, this tender Scottish diminutive — " Prince Charlie "), would require a full volume to do it justice.

Germany, too, had her poets and musicians of liberty, among whom the young Tyrtæus, Karl Theodore Koerner, stands preëminent.　This martial singer was born at Dresden, September 23, 1791, and gave great literary promise even in his youth.　By his twenty-first year he had already received the appointment of poet to the court theatre in Vienna. In 1813 France had come to the climax of her encroachments upon Germany, and in March of that year the young poet left his position to help defend his fatherland. He went to Breslau, and at once joined the Prussian Free Corps then forming under the courageous Lützow. So famous was the young recruit that, when the corps was solemnly consecrated in the church in the village of Rogau, the service was opened by the soldiers singing a lofty chorale to Koerner's own words, " *Dem Herrn allein die Ehre.*" He was now sent with Petersdorf on a mission to Dresden, to try and arouse the Saxons to unite in the common cause. Here he saw his parents for the last time. Returning to the corps in April he was at once made lieutenant by the vote of his comrades, and, a little later, was appointed Lützow's adjutant.

At Kitzen, near Leipsic, he was severely wounded, through an act of treachery, and lay in the woods during the night awaiting death. The calm courage of the man may be proved by the fact that he wrote his great " Abschied vom Leben " — " Farewell to Life " — during this dreadful night. He finally escaped to Carlsbad, but as soon as he was convalescent returned to duty. He was welcomed with enthusiasm; his poems, set to different national tunes, were sung around every camp-fire, and he had shown by his courage that they were not empty words. His pen it was that made Lützow's troop terrible to the enemy, and gave an *esprit du corps* to the soldiers that was worth many regiments.

The corps was in almost daily action. The night before August 26, 1813, Koerner seems to have had one of those foreboding moods which can often be discerned in the war-songs which are collected in his volume, entitled " Leyer und Schwert" ("Lyre and Sword "); he began the sketch of what might be called his own death-song, scribbling it in a pocket memorandum-book which he generally carried.   The next morning he was reading the poem to a brother officer when the order came to attack the French who were in the highroad in much larger force than Lützow's men.   The engagement took place between Gadebusch and Schwerin, Koerner fighting beside Lützow.   The French fled before the impetuous charge of the Free Corps.   While hotly pursuing through the woods, Koerner was shot down by a fugitive *tirailleur* who had concealed himself there. The " Song of the Sword " was found on his body ; the young poet-warrior had died on the battle-field at twenty-two.

It sounds almost as a prophecy, the fiery verse addressed to his weapon, —

> " Sword gleaming at my side,
>   Soon thou shalt be my bride."

The "Sword-song" may be called Germany's chief song of Liberty.   We attempt a translation :

SONG OF THE SWORD.

Sword at my left side gleaming
What means thy friendly beaming?
Gazest with pride on me,
Say what can the meaning be?
        Hurrah!

I am a freeman's treasure;
That fills thy sword with pleasure;
Where tyrants bar the way
There we will join the fray.
        Hurrah!

Yes, Freedom we will cherish,
Or both together perish.
Sword gleaming at my side,
Soon shalt thou be my bride.
        Hurrah!

When traitors would undo me
Be true as steel unto me.
"Oh! bridegroom do not tarry;
But say, when shall we marry?"
        Hurrah!

Mid roar and din of battle,
Mid crash and cannon rattle,
There shall our wedding be,
Then will I marry thee.
Hurrah !

" I'll wait with pulses bounding,
To hear the trumpets sounding,
Come thou to take thy maid
When roars the cannonade."
Hurrah !

Within thy scabbard ringing,
My sword, what art thou singing ?
Maiden of glittering steel,
Quickly thy thought reveal.
Hurrah !

" I'm in the scabbard clinking
Because of combat thinking.
Bridegroom, come, set me free,
I would in battle be."
Hurrah !

Though now thy case enfold thee
Right soon shall I behold thee,
Though now within thy home
Soon thou shalt to me come.
Hurrah !

" Let me not wait here sadly,
  To thee would I come gladly,
  Sighing blood-rose's breath,
  Crowned with a wreath of Death."
          Hurrah !

Then come, whate'er befalls thee,
  Thy soldier-bridegroom calls thee !
  Come forth, oh, bride adored !
  Come forth, my shining sword !
          Hurrah !

" Joy, to be newly risen,
  Joy, to have left my prison !
  Now in the rider's hand
  Glitters and gleams the brand."
          Hurrah !

No more the weapon hiding,
  For Germany we're riding ;
  Each soldier's heart aglow,
  Forward to meet the foe.
          Hurrah !

No more at left side hidden,
  To my right hand thou'rt bidden,
  There shalt thou ever be
  Till God grants Liberty.
          Hurrah !

Ne'er from my side I'll miss thee,
My iron bride, I kiss thee.
Curse him who from thee strays!
Curse him who thee betrays!
    Hurrah!

And now my bride is singing,
And hot the sparks are springing!
The morn begins to gray,
This is our wedding-day.
    Hurrah![1]

It was the wedding-day, and in a few hours after finishing this weird bridal-song its writer was dead.

Alongside of the songs of liberty, one may place, for purposes of contrast, the songs of license, the songs of that pseudo-freedom which France evolved during the Reign of Terror, and, strange to say, these songs are more intimately connected with

---

[1] Not less stirring than this song of Liberty and Death is the picture of the charge of the troop in Koerner's "Lützow's Wilde Jagd." Both poems were set to music by Germany's greatest folk-song composer — Von Weber.

American history than those thus far cited in this chapter.

One of the most peculiar features of the music of this most dreadful epoch of history is its utterly light and frivolous character. This by no means tends to make the events, which intertwined with the tunes, less gruesome, but seems to accentuate their horror. A tiny candle serves but to make darkness more impressive; the rollicking songs introduced by Shakespeare in " King Lear " or " Hamlet " but intensify the presentation of the agony of the deserted monarch, or the pathos of Ophelia's insanity. In the same manner the saturnalia of murder is made more vivid by the fact that the march played while Marie Antoinette was conducted to the guillotine was a potpourri of the most jovial opera tunes.[1]

A similar bright streak, which contrasts

[1] This march was in the possession of Mrs. Augustus Lowell, of Boston, a few years ago.

with a gloomy background, is the "Ça Ira."
It was sung to many a scene of massacre
and bloodshed; it was warbled and trilled
out when the mob carried the head of the
beautiful Princess de Lamballe, on a pike,
through the streets of Paris, and thrust it
up for the unhappy queen to look at. Yet
this melody was a light vaudeville tune,
entirely innocent in its origin, and even
patriotic in its second phase. The melody
was composed by a certain M. Bécourt, a
side-drum player at the Opéra. It very
soon became popular as a contra-dance, and
frequently appeared in the French cotillions.
We give a reproduction of this, as a lively
dance, from a collection of cotillions (in the
possession of the author) of the year 1791,
before the melody had been steeped in
blood.

The title of the work was suggested by
no less a person than Benjamin Franklin,
who, during his stay in Paris, continually

"ÇA IRA."

used the phrase (" It will succeed ") in connection with the prospects of the American
Revolution.   General Lafayette caught the
expression and suggested it to a street-
singer named Ladré, as a good refrain for
a popular song.   In its first shape it presented such innocent sentiments as these :

> " Ah !   Ça ira, ça ira, ça ira !
> Le Peuple en ce jour sans cesse répète :
> Ah !   Ça ira, ça ira, ça ira !
> Malgre les mutins, tout réussira."

But when the mob burst forth in its fury,
when the Tuileries were carried by assault,
when the nobles were massacred in prison,
then the words became more ferocious :

> " Ah !   Ça ira, ça ira, ça ira !
> Les Aristocrat' à la lanterne ;
> Ah !   Ça ira, ça ira, ça ira !
> Les Aristocrat' on les pendra."

" La Carmagnole," which was yet more
prominent during the darkest days of
France's misery, was also a light tune of

most innocent origin.[1]   It originated in the fair troubadour land of Provence.   Grétry, the French composer, thought it to be a sailor's song of Marseilles, but it was more probably a country song combined with a dance.   It had popular words attached to its measures during the early stages of the American Revolution; all the oppressed people of France were looking toward the cis-Atlantic efforts for liberty, and when the struggle began, a street-singer took up the " Carmagnole " with a new topic, beginning :

> " Bon, bon, bon,
> C'est à Boston
> Qu'on entend le bruit du Canon."

About September, 1792, there were other French topics sung to the familiar melody. The real patriots of France were now rushing forth to defend the country; the scum

[1] In Elizabeth Wormeley Latimer's excellent " Scrapbook of the French Revolution " (pp. 177 and 334), the error is made of presenting the " Carmagnole " as " Ça Ira."

had not yet risen to the top, and the third form of "La Carmagnole" was a martial one, probably written by some soldier who was ready, like Koerner, to seal his poetry with his blood.

> " Le canon vient de résonner ;
>   Guerriers soyez prêts à marcher.
>   Citoyens et soldats,
>   En volant aux combats,
>   Dansons la Carmagnole ;
>   Vive le son, vive le son,
>   Dansons la Carmagnole
>   Vive le son
>   Du Canon."

This "Carmagnole" was often sung and danced in New York during the presidency of Washington, by extreme sympathisers with the French Republic.[1]

Then there came another version, beginning :

> " Oui, je suis sans culotte, moi,
>   En dépit des amis du roi.
>   Vive les Marseillois,
>   Les Bretons et nos lois ! "

[1] Lossing's "Field-book of the War of 1812," p. 81.

But this must have existed at a time before the doctrines of the Marseillaise deputies had become too mild for such ghouls as Marat and Robespierre.

The latest amplification of the song was directed against Marie Antoinette. If the French mob disliked Louis XVI., they hated the so-called " Austrian woman " with frenzied animosity. It was believed (although this has since been disproved) that, while the king desired to help the suffering people, the queen had vetoed every measure of relief. Therefore she received the nickname of " Madame Veto." The " Carmagnole " reflected the popular feeling of '93 in all its bitterness. With its new words it was sung and danced around the guillotine while the terrible *tricoteuses* sat with their knitting, counting the falling heads, and the best blood of France was flowing. This was now the form of " La Carmagnole : "

"LA CARMAGNOLE."

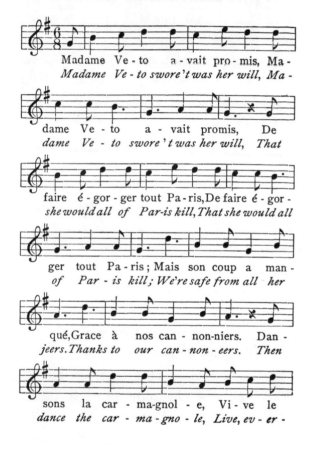

Madame Ve - to   a - vait pro - mis, Ma -
Madame Ve - to swore 't was her will, Ma -

dame Ve - to   a - vait promis,   De
dame Ve - to swore 't was her will,   That

faire é - gor - ger tout Pa - ris, De faire é - gor -
she would all of Par - is kill, That she would all

ger   tout Pa - ris; Mais son coup a   man -
of   Par - is   kill; We're safe from all   her

qué, Grace à   nos can - non-niers.   Dan -
jeers. Thanks to   our can - non - eers.   Then

sons   la car - ma-gnol - e,   Vi - ve le
dance the car - ma - gno - le,   Live, ev - er -

son, vi - ve   le son, Dansons la car - ma -
more, Live e - ver-more, Then dance the car-ma -

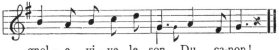

gnol - e, vi - ve le son   Du   ca-non!
gno - le, Live ev - ermore, the cannon's roar!

The "Carmagnole" was once danced and
sung even in the National Convention itself,
in November, 1793. It was when the sac-
rilegious procession of *sans-culottes* came
into the hall with the spoils of the
churches. Carlyle ("French Revolution,"
Vol. II., Book 7, Chapter IV.) thus tells of
this event :

"In such equipage did these profaners advance
toward the Convention. They enter there, in an
immense train, ranged in two rows; all masked like
mummers in fantastic sacerdotal vestments; bearing
on hand-barrows their heaped plunder — ciboriums,
suns, candelabras, plates of gold and silver.

"The address we do not give; for indeed it was
in strophes, sung *viva voce*, with all the parts; Dan-
ton, glooming considerably, in his place; and de-

manding that there be prose and decency in future. Nevertheless, the captors of such *spolia opima* crave, not untouched with liquor, permission to dance the Carmagnole also on the spot: whereto an exhilarated Convention cannot but accede.   Nay, 'several members,' continues the exaggerative Mercier, who was not there to witness, being in Limbo now, as one of Duperret's *seventy-three*, 'several members, quitting their curule chairs, took the hands of girls flaunting in Priests' vestures, and danced the Carmagnole along with them.'   Such Old-Hallowtide have they, in this year, once named of Grace, 1793."

To this picture of sacrilege may be added the scene which took place in Notre-Dame, in Paris, at the same time.   The Convention had abolished Religion and substituted an Age of Reason in its stead.   The cathedral had been assigned to the service of the new goddess of this cult.   A well-rouged goddess it was, and fitted to represent liberty of a certain kind, for Demoiselle Candeille, a dancer of the opera troupe, filled the rôle at the festival.   She was installed on the high altar of the holy church.

"Beside her stood Laharpe, the ex-Academician, the well-known author of the 'Cours de Littérature.' Holding his cap of liberty, he opened his address by denying the existence of a God; and then, blaspheming our divine Saviour, he dared Him to avenge the insult offered to Him in His temple. As no miracle took place in answer to this impious challenge, the crowd burst into loud laughter and shouts of joy. The nave of the church was then turned into a ball-room. The celebrated organist Séjan was forced to play, on the great organ, base dance-music of the period, while whirling wretches danced the Carmagnole and howled the air of 'Ça Ira.'" [1]

Infinitely nobler, more patriotic, and more dignified is the "Marseillaise." There are some songs in the world's history, which, beginning as local numbers, finally outgrow their surroundings, extend beyond the borders of even the country which bore them, and eventually become the common property of all nations. "Auld Lang Syne" was but a simple Scottish folk-melody, built on an

[1] Account by the composer Adolphe Adam, translated by Elizabeth Wormeley Latimer in *Littell's Living Age*, Aug. 23, 1879.

ancient scale of five notes only; Burns em-
bellished the old words with a few earnest
additions, and the song belongs no longer to
Scotland alone, but has become the voice of
friendship and loyalty the whole world over.
In similar manner a song composed for a
single army corps has become the universal
cry of liberty in patriotic struggles every-
where.

The " Marseillaise " was not, at its inception, intended for the Marseilles patriots.
It was composed during that early epoch of
the Revolution when France seemed to strive
only for the rights of man, and appeared as
the foe of all tyrants. It was written before
liberty degenerated into license and at the
time when true-hearted Frenchmen were
rushing forth to meet their enemies who
were springing up on every hand. Rouget
de l'Isle was in Strasburg as the army of
the lower Rhine was making itself ready to
depart for the war. Moved by the stirring

events around him, in one night, the night preceding April 24, 1792, he wrote both music and words of the great liberty hymn. The whole composition came as if by inspiration.

The originality of the melody with this composer, however, has been doubted. Castil-Blaze says that the music comes from an old German hymn ; Fétis gives an earlier French origin to it ; a rather absurd account in a recent Parisian volume [1] says :

" The melody was composed by Alexandre Boucher, the celebrated violinist, in the drawing-room of Madame de Mortaigne, at the request of a colonel whom the musician had never met before, whom he never saw again. The soldier was starting next morning with his regiment, for Marseilles, and pressed Boucher to write him a march there and then. Rouget de l'Isle, an officer of engineers, having been imprisoned in 1791 for having refused to take a second oath to the constitution, heard the march from his cell, and, at the instance of his jailer,

[1] " An Englishman in Paris." The volume is rather too sensational to be trusted, although it gives many details of Boucher's work.

adapted the words of a patriotic hymn he was then writing to it."

We are disposed to doubt all of the above; there is a tremendous amount of hazy statement and false history encrusted around many national hymns (as will be seen from the ensuing chapters), and every great melody finds a number of false claimants to its creation.

Thus much has been proved, the production was intended for the army corps of the lower Rhine, and was first called "Chant du Guerriers du Bas Rhin." But the warriors aforesaid were not greatly moved by the new effusion, and for a time it lay quiescent. These were the days when the patriots of the Assembly were becoming very impatient; the king, most woful shadow of a monarch, had endeavoured to run away and had been brought back again; the queen was entirely distrusted; the Gordian knot needed to be cut. It was then that Barbaroux, deputy from Marseilles, wrote to his city for "six hundred men who knew how to die." The stirring appeal struck home, and almost immediately the men were volunteered. Nor were they the dregs of Marseilles; history has been strangely misled regarding the character of these patriots, "*qui savent mourir;*" it has been stated over and over again that they were but the off-scourings of a maritime city; only in most recent days has an examination of municipal records established the fact that these men were respectable burghers, honest workmen, worthy tradespeople.

There were, however, not six hundred, but five hundred and sixteen, who started on the weary march northward, "to bring the tyrant to reason," although Carlyle, in his great history, erroneously adds an extra man. With three cannon, a portable forge, sledge-hammers, and pike, sword, and musket, this strange procession began its pilgrimage.

There had been a civic banquet given to wish them Godspeed. At this banquet the song composed for the army of the lower Rhine was sung. It met with a different reception from the amateur, from that which had been given it by the professional slaughterers, and it at once became the song of the battalion. Through half of France they sang it, therefore when they arrived at Paris, July 29, 1792, they were able to thunder it forth with a fervour partially derived from long practice. The Parisians were aroused to frenzy by this song of the Marseilles men.

Less than a fortnight later the melody received its baptism of blood. August 9th, in the night-time, the tocsin sounded for the attack on the Tuileries, and on the 10th the " Marseillaise " blended with the dying shrieks of the Swiss Guards.

The " Marseillaise " was heard again under very different circumstances; the evil days were hurrying on, the scum was rising. In a short time the mob of *sans-culottes* found the patriotic hymn too conservative for their fury, and the " Carmagnole " and " Ça Ira " became the popular music. But the " Marseillaise " still stood as the chosen song of the men who loved Liberty without committing crimes in her name. These men were, however, proscribed and hunted down, and Oct. 30, 1793, twenty-two of the Girondins (as the moderates were called) were tried for their "treason," among them that Brissot de Warville who had spoken so well of the music of Boston.

Those were the days of short deliberations; the entire band was quickly sentenced to death. Valazé at once struck a dagger into his heart and fell dead.[1] The others, as they were led back to prison, sang the " Marseillaise." They were all to

[1] His body was beheaded with the Girondins, the next day.

die on the morrow. Vergniaud had poison concealed on his person, but a rapid calculation proved that there was not enough for all, and he therefore threw it away. Poet, painter, and historian have celebrated that wonderful night when the greatest minds in France had their final reunion before their execution; there was wit without bravado, courage without braggadocio, serenity among all.

The next day they took up their song of the " Marseillaise " at the guillotine. Swiftly the instrument did its dreadful work; one by one the voices were hushed ; at last there was but one firm voice singing the patriotic air, and in an instant that, too, was stilled, and the tragedy of the Girondins had come to its close.

Barbaroux, himself, who might be called the godfather of the " Marseillaise," was proscribed, but managed to escape. He found refuge in St. Emilion. One day, in 1794, he saw a crowd approaching his hiding-place; he drew a pistol and shot himself. It was only a crowd of harvesters making festival, the "Terror" was coming to its end, and Barbaroux was safe, had he only known it.

Of the composer of the "Marseillaise" it must be added that he was by no means true to the principles of his great song, for he afterward composed Legitimist, Royalist, and Imperialist songs, but we may easily imagine these to have sprung from his empty pocket-book, rather than from his heart.

Of the power of his song there can be no manner of doubt. A certain left-handed compliment may serve to show this; when Rouget de l'Isle was presented to Klopstock, the celebrated German writer turned from him, exclaiming: "Monster! your music has killed fifty thousand Germans!" De l'Isle was again imprisoned during the Reign of Terror, but the death of Robespierre relieved him from this great peril. Louis Philippe

granted him a pension because of the
" Marseillaise."

Probably the national song that has been
put to the most diverse uses by more civi-
lised nations than had ever before united
upon a single tune, is "God Save the
Queen." The English national anthem has
become a patriotic song in Germany, used
since 1793, under the title of " Heil dir im
Siegerkranz ;" it has been adopted in Switzerland, and it has had many different American and other settings. Before examining
these, let us trace, as far as possible, the
origin of the music. As is the case with
many of the greatest national anthems, the
beginning of the melody is ascribed to different sources, and the historians are still
breaking lances in favour of different theories
regarding its origin.

Briefly stated, some of the different views
are the following :

1st, An old air, by Dr. John Bull, dated

1619, very much resembles the modern tune, but it is in a minor key.

2d, A Scottish carol, in a Ravenscroft collection, entitled " Remember, O thou man," bears a strong resemblance to the tune, both in its form and progressions, but is also in minor.

3d, A ballad entitled " Franklin Is Fled Away," dated 1669, is in the form, and is in major, but deviates from the melody.

4th, A harpsichord piece by Henry Purcell, dated 1696, bears resemblance to the last half of the melody.

5th, It is claimed, but not proved, that the tune and words were written for King James II., and that it was sung by the Catholic chapel of that king.

6th, It is claimed as a Jacobite song, written for James III., the " Old Pretender."

7th, It is claimed that Lully, the old French composer, wrote the tune.[1]

[1] Three nuns of the convent of St. Cyr, Chartres, have testified to the existence of the tune at that convent in

We might give several more claims to the work, but we have cited enough to show how speedily pseudo-historical tales cluster around national music.   There seems, however, scarcely to be a doubt that Henry Carey, the composer of "Sally in our Alley," the unfortunate genius who committed suicide after a blameless life of eighty years, who died with a single halfpenny in his pocket, was the author and composer of the great anthem.   It was at a tavern in Cornhill, in 1740, at a meeting convened to celebrate the capture of Porto Bello, that the song was first heard, the singer being Henry Carey, who, after being heartily applauded, announced that it was (both words and music) his *own composition*.[1]   There are

the last century.   An article recently appeared in the *Saturday Review* of Mobile, Ala., on this subject, contributed by Prof. Paul J. Robert.   Grove's "Dictionary of Music and Musicians" also alludes to the Lully theory; but it is only another instance of family resemblance among popular melodies.

[1] See *Gentleman's Magazine*, 1796; Chappell's "Na-

HENRY CAREY

many witnesses to this fact, and the idea that Carey could have purloined so striking a melody without being detected may be dismissed as absurd. The resemblances alluded to above are undoubtedly existent, but they prove nothing. Any great national song, intended to be performed by great masses of singers, often untrained, must be of simple construction;[1] and "God Save Great George, our King" was almost entirely in conjunct movement, scarcely any skips occurring in the melody. Its entire compass is less than an octave, a very great merit. Such a tune, however, will always bear a family resemblance to many others. The chief theme of the finale of Beethoven's ninth symphony, for example, is as close to

tional English Airs," p. 86; Cummings's articles in the *Musical Times*, March to August, 1878; and the essay in the first volume of Chrysander's "Jahrbücher."

[1] That the "Star-spangled Banner" and "Hail Columbia" are not so, is due to the fact that they were not originally national or patriotic songs.

" Yankee Doodle " as any of the before-cited
tunes are to " God Save the King," yet
nobody has yet accused the great symphonist
of stealing the American melody. It is
finical folly to dwell upon such resemblances as having any historical impor-
tance.

The singable character of the English
national anthem was at once proved by two
events. Firstly, the whole nation began singing it and paid to the anthem a respect equal
to that accorded to the English flag. Haydn,
during his two visits to London (1791 and
1794–95), was so impressed by this fact that
he determined to write an anthem for his own
country on his return to Austria, and, in
January, 1797, together with the poet
Hauschka, he produced " Gott erhalte Franz
den Kaiser," a weaker dynastic ode, but also
only a version of England's national anthem
strained through a German mind. It may be
added, however, that this is the only example

of a national hymn being composed with a predetermination to that effect.

The second circumstance which proved the suitability of the English melody to its purpose was the fact that it was very soon appropriated right and left in various countries and by different composers. Weber and Beethoven used it, both more than once; it became a Danish national air, then Prussia appropriated it, and before this, America, even while fighting with the mother country, was not averse to using the English national anthem as an American song.

It is generally supposed that " My Country, 'tis of Thee " was the only employment of the old melody by Americans. Such is not, however, the case. Almost immediately after the Revolution, the music of "God Save the King" was heard to the poetry of local patriotism. Among the earliest [1] settings was the following :

[1] There was also a set of patriotic verses to the tune, published in the *Pennsylvania Packet* at Philadelphia in 1779.

"ODE FOR THE FOURTH OF JULY.

" Come all ye sons of Song,
  Pour the full sound along
    In joyful strains.
  Beneath these western skies
  See a new Empire rise,
  Bursting with glad surprise
    Tyrannic chains.

" Liberty with keen eye,
  Pierced the blue vaulted sky,
    Resolved us free.
  From her imperial seat,
  Beheld the bleeding state,
  Approved this day's debate
    And firm decree."

After other verses in this bombastic style,
the final stanza is reached in the following
burst :

" Now all ye sons of Song,
  Pour the full sound along,
    Who shall control;
  For in this western clime,
  Freedom shall rise sublime,
  Till ever-changing time,
    Shall cease to roll."

Nor was this the only employment of the singable theme. The love of high-sounding metaphor and hyperbole, which ruled the lesser poets of the post-revolutionary epoch, can be best shown by quoting the most striking parts of a poem, (now in possession of the author) evolved, to the English music, in 1786 or 1787:

" An ode, written by Thomas Dawes, jun. esquire, and sung at the entertainment given on Bunker's Hill, by the proprietors of Charles River Bridge, at the opening of the same.

> " Now let rich music sound,
> And all the region round,
>   With rapture fill;
> Let the shrill trumpet's fame,
> To heaven itself proclaim,
> The ever-lasting name
>   Of Bunker's Hill.

> " Beneath his sky-rapt brow,
> What heroes sleep below,
>   How dear to Jove.
> Not more beloved were those,
> Who soiled celestial foes,
> When the old giants rose
>   To arms above.

" Now scarce eleven short years,
  Have rolled their rapid spheres,
    Thro' heaven's high road,
  Since o'er yon swelling tide,
  Passed all the British pride,
  And watered Bunker's side
    With foreign blood.

" Then Charlestown's gilded spires,
  Met unrelenting fires,
    And sunk in night :
  But Phenix like they'll rise,
  In columns to the skies,
  And strike the astonished eyes
    With glories bright.

" Meandering to the deep
  Majestic Charles shall weep
    Of war no more ;
  Famed as the Appian way,
  The world's first bridge to-day,
  All nations shall convey,
    From shore to shore."

One is a little astounded at the poetic
license of the writer ; the "sky-rapt brow"
of the hill is not higher than some of the

spires in the town, the Appian way still remains the more famous of the two structures,
and even now the bridge from Boston to
Charlestown is not conveying " all nations "
from " shore to shore," nor does Charlestown [1] (sometimes irreverently called " Pig-
town " by unregenerate youth) yet rise " in
columns to the skies, and strike the astonished eyes with glories bright."

With the American of the present, however, the chief employment of the English
national hymn is found in the singing of
" My Country, 'tis of Thee," which has
received the name of " America." This
popular setting of the old English melody is
due to a Baptist clergyman, Rev. Samuel F.
Smith, who was born in Boston, Oct. 21,
1808. Mr. Smith was a very facile writer,
editor of numerous religious publications,
professor at the Waterville (Maine) College,

[1] Charlestown is now incorporated with the city of
Boston.

now known as Colby College, which con-
ferred the degree of " D. D." upon him ; but
it is by his patriotic poem that he is known
throughout the country.   This effusion was
written while Mr. Smith was a theological
student at Andover, in 1832.   It was first
sung at a children's celebration in Park
Street Church, in Boston, July 4, 1832.   It
immediately became popular.   Oliver Wendell Holmes was a classmate of Doctor Smith
at Harvard, in the famous class of 1829, and
at a reunion of the graduates, long after,
summed up the clergyman's title to fame,
very neatly, as follows :

" And there's a nice youngster of excellent pith,
    Fate tried to conceal him by naming him Smith !
    But he chanted a song for the brave and the free,
    Just read on his medal — ' My Country of Thee.' "

CHAPTER V.

"YANKEE DOODLE" is shrouded in mystery; glib derivations of its tune are given
on every hand, but when sifted many of these
statements are found to belong to the realm
of guesswork or tradition, rather than of
history. The haziness of the entire subject begins, at the very threshold, with its
title.

The word " Yankee" has been a bone of
contention for generations among etymolo-
gists. Among the investigators of this topic
none has devoted himself more assiduously to

tracing the various tales to their source than Mr. Albert Matthews, of Boston, who we trust will some day write a monograph upon the subject, and who has aided the author greatly in compiling the following data.

The word "Yankee" seems almost always to have been applied to New Englanders, and was generally a term of mild sarcasm; yet one authority makes the word to be an adjective expressing excellence. It is said to have been thus used by "Yankee Hastings," of Cambridge, in 1713, he employing the expressions, "A Yankee horse," "A Yankee team," as superlatives.

Probably the most generally accepted origin of the word is that the Indians applied it to the white settlers in New England, in a vain effort to say "Anglois" or "English." This theory derives some inferential support from the fact that the Indians had much difficulty in pronouncing the letter "L."

Governor Edward Winslow, in his book entitled "Good News from New England" (London, 1624), states that the Indians were always obliged to call him "Winsnow," through their inability to pronounce the aforesaid letter.

Another authority states that "Eankke" in one of the Indian dialects means a coward, and that the New Englanders were thus called by the Virginians because they refused to assist them against the Cherokees.

One authority, whose imagination would certainly give him good rank among some of the Shakesperian commentators, suggests that the word might be a corruption of "Yorkshire."

Another states that the English, having conquered a tribe of Indians called the "Yankoos," received the name of that tribe, "according to Indian custom." As no tribe of that name has yet been discovered, and as the " custom " itself has not been verified, this may be regarded as a very far-fetched theory.

Another commentator suggests that the name came from the Dutch settlers, who called the New Englanders "Jannekin" ("Johnnie"), in patronising sarcasm. This is at least a possible solution.

The whole term, "Yankee Doodle," has also been derived from the Persian "Yanghi Dunia" or the Turkish "Yankee Dooniah," applied to this country and its inhabitants, but we imagine that investigation will prove that the derivation should be traced in the opposite direction. George Kennan, the celebrated traveller, once stated to the author that, on his second trip through the Caucasus, he found the natives to have taken up many of his American songs, which he had sung to them with banjo accompaniment, and orientalised them. Some day the commentators will find these songs and prove some of our music of Asiatic origin, exactly as the above-mentioned commentators derive "Yankee Doodle" from an Asiatic "Yanghi Dunia."

The word "Yankee" is also derived from the Norwegian and other languages.

"Doodle" has been traced to the Lancashire dialect, as meaning a trifler, a shiftless fellow; but it is by no means certain that it is thus used in the American song. Apart from the application of the nickname to "Yankee Hastings," mentioned above, the word "Yankee" first definitely appears as a negro name, in 1725.

Thus much of the etymology; in tracing the origin of the tune of the song, one is met with fully as many theories and an overwhelming amount of unproved and guesswork history. Here are a few of the theories: "Yankee Doodle" is said to have been a derisive song against Oliver Cromwell, beginning, "Nankie Doodle came to town."

This has not been traced in the slightest degree; the whole story is apocryphal.

It has been said that the melody was first used in the time of Charles II. to the words,

> "Lucy Locket lost her pocket,
> Kitty Fisher found it,
> Not a bit of money in it,
> Only binding round it."

It is true that this nursery rhyme fits well to the melody, but Lucy Locket is evidently a name taken from the "Beggar's Opera," written in 1727, and Kitty Fischer (as the name was spelled) died in 1771, which removes the matter a half century and more beyond the reign of Charles II.

Thirdly, it has been stated that the tune is sung in Holland, generally by the harvesters, and that it might have come thence. Spite of the ridicule that has been thrown upon this theory, we can state that part of the tune is well known in the Netherlands, although, as yet, its antiquity is not ascertained. This simple fact has been overlaid by considerable nonsense. One investigator, (?) [1] for example, gives the following words as the regular Dutch version of the song :

> " Yanker didel, doodel, down ;
> Didel, dudel, lanter,
> Yanke viver, voover vown
> Botermilk and tather."

Which is consummate gibberish and belongs to no known language. It is probable that the silly lines were invented out of the whole cloth, as an appendix to the fact that the Dutch possess the melody.

Just as this volume is going to press the author is enabled, through the kindness of M. Jules Koopman, travelling in Holland, to trace this theory of Dutch origin more definitely. The *first period* of the melody is quite familiar to Dutch musicians, and has been used in Holland from time immemorial

[1] *Littell's Living Age*, August, 1861.

as a *children's song;* the second period is
not known in Holland. There is a possi-
bility, therefore, that the English country
dance (quoted a little later on) was elabo-
rated from a Dutch nursery-song, or it may
be another of the accidental resemblances
with which music is so copiously strewn.

There are also the usual "resemblance"
theories, which would give the tune a Span-
ish and even a Hungarian origin. The following note is from a secretary of legation,
at Madrid : [1]

"The tune 'Yankee Doodle,' from the first of my
showing it here, has been acknowledged by persons
acquainted with music to bear a strong resemblance
to the popular airs of Biscay; and yesterday, a professor from the north recognised it as being much
like the ancient sword dance played on solemn occasions by the people of San Sebastian. He says the
tune varies in those provinces, and proposes in a
couple of months to give me the changes as they are
to be found in their different towns, that the matter
may be judged of and fairly understood. Our national

[1] Quoted by Nason, " Our National Song," p. 20.

air certainly has its origin in the music of the free Pyrenees; the first strains are identically those of the heroic " Danza Esparta," as it was played to me, of brave old Biscay.

" Very truly yours,
" BUCKINGHAM SMITH.

" *Madrid, June 3, 1858.*"

But there is no record of the further investigation promised above ever having been made.

It is stated that Louis Kossuth, when in this country, recognised the melody as resembling one of the tunes of his fatherland.

And now to leave the realm of supposition, and study what is definitely discovered regarding this merry theme. There are few early printed editions of the melody; it occurs in George Colman's opera (printed in 1784), entitled "Two to One." The music of this was selected and arranged, although the title-page says "composed," by Doctor Arnold. In this work is a song entitled "Adzooks, Old Crusty, Why so Rusty?"[1]

[1] See Appendix.

which is the tune of "Yankee Doodle."
W. Barclay Squire, in an article in Grove's
"Dictionary of Music and Musicians," thinks
this to be the earliest appearance of the tune
in print, but Frank Kidson, in his "Old
English Country Dances" (p. 34), says:

"I believe the set I now give is, at least, eight or
nine years previous. It is from 'A Selection of
Scotch, English, Irish, and Foreign Airs — Glasgow,
James Aird, Vol. I.' Oblong 16mo. It is unfortunately not dated, but I cannot find any air in it which
gives a later date than 1775 or 1776, and I fix its
publication at about that period." [1]

We append the version which Mr. Kidson
presents.

"YANKY DOODLE."

[1] See Appendix.

Of course it is definitely known that the air was freely used both by English and Americans long before these printed versions. Yet when one endeavours to ascertain the beginnings of the tune in America the mists of fiction immediately arise.

The following is an example of the bold way in which history (?) is sometimes made; the extract is from *Farmer & Moore's Monthly Literary Journal:*

"In looking over an old file of the *Albany Statesman*[1] we met the following interesting note respecting the origin of the tune 'Yankee Doodle,' the words of which were published in the collection for May. It is a fact that the British army lay encamped in the summer of 1755, on the eastern bank of the Hudson, a little south of the city of Albany. To this day vestiges of their encampment remain, and, after a lapse of sixty years, the inquisitive traveller can observe the remains of the ashes, the places where they boiled their camp kettles, etc. In the early part of June the eastern troops began to pour in, company

[1] This in itself is an error, since no such paper existed at that time. The *Albany Register* or the *New York Statesman* is probably meant.

after company, and such a motley assemblage of men
never before thronged together on such an occasion.
It would, said my worthy ancestor, who relates to me
the story, have relaxed the gravity of an anchorite to
have seen the descendants of the Puritans making
through the streets of our ancient city to take their
station on the left of the British army, some with
long coats.   Their march, their accoutrements, and
the whole arrangement of their troops furnished matter of amusement to the wits of the British army.
Among the club of wits that belonged to the British
army there was a physician attached to the staff, by
the name of Doctor Shackburg, who combined with
the science of the surgeon the skill and talents of a
musician.   To please Brother Jonathan he composed
a tune, and, with much gravity, recommended it to
the officers as one of the most celebrated airs of
martial musick.   The joke took, to the no small
amusement of the British Corps.   Brother Jonathan
exclaimed that it was ' 'nation fine,' and in a few
days nothing was heard in the provincial camp but
' Yankee Doodle ! ' "

Thus the first claim for Doctor Shuckburgh is made on uncorroborated testimony,
about sixty years after the event.

Faulty as the above account is, one may
find grains of truth here and there.   It is

probable (since many traditions agree on this) that the witty doctor arranged a melody or song, either for, or about, the uncouth troops that were coming into Albany. Many of the accounts attach him to General Abercrombie's staff, but this could not be if the tune or the adaptation was made in 1755.[1] It is probable that the surgeon was with General Amherst when the New England troops under Gov. William Shirley came in. The probability is that he took an old English tune (it bears every internal evidence of having been a country dance) and set it as a satirical song. The name of the doctor is given in a half dozen different ways. " Schuckburgh " (Grove's Dictionary), " Shackburg " (*vide* account above), " Shackbergh " (in letter following), " Shackleford," " Shukberg," and other variants occur. The proper spelling is " Shuckburgh," for he

[1] General Abercrombie came to this country in the spring of 1756.

wrote it thus himself, and his friend, Sir William Johnson, always wrote it the same. A New York paper (the *New York Gazetteer*) of Aug. 26, 1773, contains the following :

> " Died, at Schenectady, last Monday, Dr. Richard Shuckburgh, a gentleman of a very genteel family, and of infinite jest and humour."

A granddaughter of Gen. Robert Van Rensselaer writes thus regarding the story of "Yankee Doodle," to Albert Matthews, Esq., of Boston :

> " The story of ' Yankee Doodle ' is an authentic tradition in my family.   My grandfather, Brig.-Gen. Robert Van Rensselaer, born in the Greenbush Manor House, was a boy of seventeen at the time when Doctor Shackbergh, the writer of the verses, and General Abercrombie were guests of his father, Col. Johannes Van Rensselaer, in June, 1758.   The room which Doctor Shackbergh occupied was always pointed out to the children of the family, who felt a certain kind of proprietorship in the famous ' Yankee Doodle.'   The school children in Albany know the old house and its story ; teachers have long been in the habit of making it a place of pilgrimage for their classes.   There is no room for doubt in my

mind that Doctor Shackbergh wrote the lines attributed to him. And the place and date have long
been so fixed a fact in my family that I am equally
convinced of the accuracy of the report of the last
two generations. All that we claim for Fort Crailo
is that it was the birthplace of the original composition. There was a verse in a harvest-song used in
Holland, sung, it is said, to this tune, several hundred
years ago [!] where the words ' Yanker, didel, dudel '
[so this lady was also caught by the weak newspaper
rigmarole] may have given the text for later expan-
sion."

After alluding to the supposed fact that
the melody was used as a satire against
Cromwell, the lady continues her interesting,
but by no means convincing letter :

"We have a picture of the old house as it was
before the Revolution, and in the rear is the old well,
with the high stone curb and well-sweep which has
always been associated with the lines written while
the British surgeon sat upon the curb. We hope to
restore the curb as it was."

Almost every investigation into the early
American stages of " Yankee Doodle " leads
us to similar reports of traditions. Yet where
these traditions corroborate each other it may

not be too trusting to pin one's faith upon
some original occurrence as above described.
It is highly probable that Doctor Shuckburgh did write a satirical poem to a dance-
tune with which he was familiar, and that
the result was " Yankee Doodle." It has
been often stated that the lines written
against Cromwell (which are probably entirely fictitious as connected with the Protector) ran thus :

> " Nankie Doodle came to town
> On a little pony,
> Stuck a feather in his cap
> And called him Macaroni."

It is, however, more likely that Doctor
Shuckburgh wrote words like these, for the
word " Macaroni " at about this time (1755)
meant something like the " Dude " of to-day,
and the whole stanza (altering the first word
to " Yankee ") would suit admirably to satirise the New England regiments which
aroused the wit's risibility.

Again, it may be accepted that the song was *against* the Americans at first, and this point we shall now emphasise by citing many of its uses. At first we find it only among the English. Here is the earliest notice of its performance :

" The British fleet was bro't to anchor near Castle William, in Boston Harbor, and the opinion of the visitors to the ships was that the ' Yankey Doodle Song' was the capital piece in the band of their musicians." — *New York Journal*, Oct. 13, 1768.

The same band that played the " Yankey Doodle Song " at this time, also gave the Bostonians better music, but " Yankee Doodle " seems to have taken root immediately, and was often played in the streets of Boston thereafter. It began and ended the American Revolution, as we shall presently see.

Undoubtedly the word " Yankee " was now used as opprobrium ; in the evidence regarding the Boston massacre, we find that the British commanding officer shouted the word at the mob with other contemptuous expressions.

Unfortunately, the tune of "Yankee Doodle" cannot be traced in its performances between 1755 and 1768, and even after the latter date no one seems to have thought of writing up the history or origin of the song.   But the Bostonians and their neighbours heard it often enough during the years immediately following.   The British troops began to sing it in derision of the Americans.   The soldiers had been made to feel that they had no business in Boston, and they took revenge in such ways as lay at their disposal.   Knowing the religious disposition of many of the Bostonians, the troops would often race horses on the Common on Sundays or cause their bands to play "Yankee Doodle" just outside of the church doors.[1]

[1] Fiske's " American Revolution," Vol. I., p. 65.

A little later, when the camps were in the town of Boston, the British custom was to drum culprits out of camp to the tune of "Yankee Doodle," a decidedly jovial " Cantio in exitu." Still later we find the soldiers making ribald verses to the melody and singing :

> " Yankee Doodle came to town
> For to buy a firelock ;
> We will tar and feather him
> And so we will John Hancock."

But the musical prologue to the Revolution was played when Lord Percy marched out of Boston to the relief of Colonel Smith and Major Pitcairn, who were in great stress at Lexington.[1] That surely was the overture to the great drama that was beginning. The Americans immediately appropriated the tune and for a long time it was called " The Lexington March." It may be of interest, in this connection, to know what music cheered

[1] " History of Lexington," Hudson, pp. 197–98, and Fiske's " American Revolution," Vol. I., p. 124.

the other side.   The fife and drum attached
to Colonel Pickering's regiment, as it marched
from Salem to Lexington, April 19, 1775,
played a tune called " The Black Sloven."
It is preserved in an old book of manuscript music still existing in the Essex Institute at Salem.   It is as follows :

COL. PICKERING'S MARCH TO LEXINGTON.

It will be seen that neither side had much
advantage in the quality of its music.

But the subject of national music ought
not to be finally judged by the analytical
tests of the technical musician.   When a

man hears a melody in a foreign land, or in the midst of a battle (with a ground-bass of shot and shell), he will care very little for the historian who coldly tells him that the tune did not originate with his nation, or the contrapuntist who haughtily explains that it is very trashy music; it represents the land he loves, and that is enough. Many a man thinks he is being thrilled by music, when he is really being moved by memories.

Yet, if we subject our national melodies to strict musical or historical tests the result is unsatisfactory.

Richard Grant White, although making many errors in his historical statements regarding American national music, is not altogether wrong, although needlessly harsh, when he speaks of our three chief melodies as follows : [1]

[1] "National Hymns: how they are written and how they are not written," pp. 18–22.

"As a patriotic song for the people at large, as a national hymn, the 'Star-spangled Banner' was found to be almost useless. The range of the air, an octave and a half, places it out of the compass of ordinary voices ; and no change that has been made in it has succeeded in obviating this paramount objection, without depriving the music of that characteristic spirit which is given by its quick ascent through such an extended range of notes.[1]

"The words, too, are altogether unfitted for a national hymn. They are almost entirely descriptive, and of a particular event. . . . The lines are also too long and the rhyme too involved for a truly patriotic song. They tax the memory ; they should aid it.

"The rhythm, too, is complicated, and often harsh and vague. . . . In fact, only the choral lines of this song have brought it into general favour.

"'And the star-spangled banner in triumph shall wave
O'er the land of the free and the home of the brave.'

"But even in regard to this, who cannot but wish that the spangles could be taken out, and a good, honest flag be substituted for the banner?

"'The Star-spangled Banner,' though for these reasons so utterly inadequate to the requirements of a national hymn that the people stood mute while in some instances it was sung by a single voice, or in

---

[1] This came from its original use as a drinking song.

most cases it was only played by a band, is yet far the best of the three songs, which, for lack of better, have until now been called American national airs.

" Of the other two, ' Yankee Doodle ' has the claim of long association, and will probably always retain a certain degree of a certain kind of favour. But no sane person would ever dream of regarding it as a national hymn. Its words, as all know who have ever heard them, are mere childish burlesque; and its air, if air it must be called, is as comical as its words, and can scarcely be regarded as being properly music. . . . ' Hail Columbia ' is really worse than ' Yankee Doodle.' That has a character, although it is comic; and it is respectable, because it makes no pretence. But both the words and the music of ' Hail Columbia ' are commonplace, vulgar, and pretentious; and the people themselves have found all this out."

For all this fierce indictment, we fancy that " Yankee Doodle," especially in its words, may hold its own beside the song which won the English Revolution — " Lilli-burlero."

Through the remainder of our Revolution " Yankee Doodle " was frankly accepted by the Americans as their own. It had been the prelude to the war, it became also its postlude.

At the surrender of Lord Cornwallis at Yorktown, in 1781, there came up a peculiar matter of music for decision.[1] The Americans had been lenient in many of the details of the surrender, but on one point they were inflexible. The British had always made it a point to demand, at the surrender of an enemy, that the bands of the captives should play their national music, thus humiliating the conquered by dragging their melody in the dust with them. They had exacted this of the American general, Lincoln, at the surrender of Charleston. And now the American who was conducting the negotiations, Colonel Laurens, directed that Lord Cornwallis's sword should be received by General Lincoln, and that the army, on marching out to lay down its arms, should play either a British or a German air. The

[1] See Fiske's "American Revolution," Vol. II., p. 283.

latter alternative was to humiliate the Hessians. There was no help for it. On the nineteenth of October Cornwallis's army, 7,247 in number, with 840 seamen, marched out with colours furled and cased, their bands playing an old English tune entitled "The World Turned Upside Down," which they undoubtedly thought appropriate to the occasion. The American bands now played "Yankee Doodle."

It was a long time after this that Europe heard "Yankee Doodle" as an American anthem. After the War of 1812 this also came about. It was in 1814 that Henry Clay and John Quincy Adams met the British ambassador at Ghent to arrange the final points and to sign the treaty of peace between Great Britain and America.[1] The burghers of the city were proud that

[1] The treaty was signed Dec. 24, 1814. The citizens of Ghent (whose sympathies were with the Americans) rejoiced greatly. Lossing's "Fieldbook of the War of 1812," p. 1061.

the event should have taken place within their walls, and on the day of the signing proposed a serenade to the two embassies. They knew the English tune well enough, but what was the American national hymn?[1] In much perplexity the bandmaster went to Henry Clay to inquire about it. Of course he was told that our chief national melody was "Yankee Doodle." As he did not know the tune he begged Mr. Clay to hum

[1] Although this story has been current since Clay's time, it requires some emendation. The people of Ghent certainly knew of one American tune at this time, — "Hail Columbia;" for this was performed on the twenty-seventh of October, 1814, when the Academy of Sciences and Fine Arts of Ghent invited the American commissioners to attend their exercises. A sumptuous dinner followed, at which the chief magistrate of Ghent offered the following toast, "Our distinguished guests and fellow-members, the American ministers, — may they succeed in making an honourable peace to secure the liberty and independence of their country," after which the band played "Hail Columbia." The British commissioners were not present at this meeting. It is probable that the bandmaster above mentioned wished to play several American airs to fill out the proper length of a serenade, and that this led to the whistling of "Yankee Doodle" as stated.

it to him that he might note it down. Clay
tried and failed; the secretary of legation
tried to warble the melody and also came
to grief. Finally, Clay rose to the emergency; calling his body-servant he said,
"Bob, whistle 'Yankee Doodle' to this
gentleman," and from the lips of that
musical darkey the first European tran-
scription of the tune as an American
national song was made. It was quickly
harmonised, copied, and the serenade took
place as designed.

In summing up the various theories regarding "Yankee Doodle," we regret that it
is impossible to reach the domain of certainty; its origin still remains shrouded in
mystery. Inferential proof, however, seems
to show that it was an old English country
dance, partially resembling an old Dutch children's song; that Doctor Shuckburgh used
it to satirise the New Englanders; that it
was a British tune at the beginning of the

Revolution, an American melody at its end ; and that it very soon lost its local, New England application, and became entirely national.

CHAPTER VI.

"Hail Columbia" — Originally an Instrumental Composition — "The President's March" — Doubts about the Composer.

IF an American were asked the name of his national anthem, he would probably pass by the rollicking "Yankee Doodle," and the bombastic "Hail Columbia," and acknowledge only the "Star-spangled Banner." In Europe they have decided the matter differently. It is necessary, on state occasions abroad, when music plays its part in festivities, to know definitely what melody to perform as compliment to each nation. On such occasions the European bands play "Hail Columbia" as their homage to the United States. It was played, in such manner, when the first American war-ship passed through the canal at Kiel, in Germany, and when Edison entered the Paris Grand Opera House, in 1889, it was "Hail Columbia" which conveyed the homage of the French people to America in the person of the great electrician.

Yet "Hail Columbia" has become the most threadbare of our national songs; it is a representative of a bygone epoch of braggadocio and extreme hyperbole; it is as hopelessly antiquated as the Fourth of July Song, or the Ode upon the opening of a bridge, printed in a preceding chapter. Yet it remains interesting as a realistic picture of its time.   It arose in a manner which in itself would forbid its being an art work of highest class; the cart, in this case, was put before the horse, the music written long before the words, the poetry forced upon the tune afterward.

During the Revolution there was a very tawdry march often played by the American

bands, entitled "The Washington March."
When Washington was elected the first
President of the United States, some musician hit on the idea of composing something
better to celebrate the event and for performance on public occasions thenceforward.

Again we find the conflicting stories
connected with the composition which seem
to accompany almost every successful piece
of national music. To state the ascertained
facts first; it is definitely known that the
composition was written in 1789, and that
it was called "The President's March."
Regarding its first performance and its
composer there is some doubt. William
McKoy, in "Poulson's Advertiser" for 1829,
states that the march was composed by a
German musician in Philadelphia, named
Johannes Roth. He is also called "Roat"
and "Old Roat," in some accounts. That
there was a Philip Roth living in Philadelphia at about this time may be easily proved,

for his name is found in the city directories
from 1791 to 1799.[1]   He appears as " Roth,
Philip, teacher of music, 25 Crown St."
Washington at this time was a fellow citizen
of this musician, for he lived at 190 High
Street, Philadelphia.

But there is another claimant to the work.
There was also in Philadelphia at this
time a German musician, whose name is
spelled in many different ways by the commentators.   He is called " Phyla," " Philo,"
" Pfylo," and " Pfyles," by various authors.
None of these seems like a German name,
but it is possible that the actual name may
have been " Pfeil."[2]   This gentleman of
doubtful cognomen claims the authorship

[1] " History of the Flag of the United States," by Rear-
Admiral Geo. Henry Preble, p. 719.

[2] Through the courtesy of John W. Jordan, Esq.,
librarian of the Historical Society of Pennsylvania, we
learn that the first Philadelphia " City Directory" was
published in 1785, the second in 1791.   In neither of
these does the name of any musician bearing any resemblance to the ones given above appear.

JOSEPH HOPKINSON.

of the march in question, or rather his son has claimed it for him. The march is also claimed by this son to have been first played on Trenton Bridge as Washington rode over, on his way to the New York inauguration. Richard Grant White, however, states, on what authority we know not, that the work was first played on the occasion of a visit of Washington to the old John Street Theatre in New York.[1]

But "The President's March" would eventually have died a natural death, had it not suddenly received an accession of patriotic words. These words were written by J. Hopkinson, Esq., who afterward became the Hon. Joseph Hopkinson, LL.D.,

[1] "National Hymns," p. 22, foot-note. But in this paragraph, R. G. White is altogether too omniscient. He brushes away the most disputed points with comical terseness. "The 'Star-spangled Banner,' is an old French air," . . . "'Yankee Doodle' is an old English air," — are specimens of this dismissal of doubtful topics by the literary autocrat. It may be good critical, but it is very poor historical, writing.

vice-president of the American Philosophical Society, president of the Pennsylvania Academy of Fine Arts, etc. As to the writing of the words, we can have no better authority than Doctor Hopkinson himself, and we therefore quote a letter written to Rev. Rufus W. Griswold, a short time before Hopkinson's death:

"'Hail Columbia' was written in the summer of 1798, when war with France was thought to be inevitable. Congress was then in session in Philadelphia, debating upon that important subject, and acts of hostility had actually taken place. The contest between England and France was raging, and the people of the United States were divided into parties for the one side or the other, some thinking that policy and duty required us to espouse the cause of 'republican France,' as she was called, while others were for connecting ourselves with England, under the belief that she was the great preservative power of good principles and safe government. The violation of our rights by both belligerents was forcing us from the just and wise policy of President Washington, which was to do equal justice to both but to take part with neither, and to preserve an honest and strict neutrality between them. The prospect of a

rupture with France was exceedingly offensive to the
portion of the people who espoused her cause, and
the violence of the spirit of party has never risen
higher, I think not so high, in our country, as it did
at that time upon that question. The theatre was
then open in our city. A young man belonging to it,
whose talent was high as a singer, was about to take
a benefit. I had known him when he was at school.
On this acquaintance he called on me one Saturday
afternoon, his benefit being announced for the following Monday. His prospects were very disheart-
ening; but he said that if he could get a patriotic
song adapted to ' The President's March,' he did not
doubt of a full house ; that the poets of the theatrical
corps had been trying to accomplish it, but had not
succeeded. I told him I would try what I could do
for him. He came the next afternoon, and the song,
such as it is, was ready for him. The object of the
author was to get up an American spirit which should
be independent of, and above the interests, passion,
and policy of both belligerents, and look and feel
exclusively for our honour and rights. No allusion is
made to France or England, or the quarrel between
them, or to the question which was most in fault in
their treatment of us. Of course the song found
favour with both parties, for both were American,
at least neither could disown the sentiments and feelings it indicated. Such is the history of this song,
which has endured infinitely beyond the expectation
of the author, as it is beyond any merit it can boast

of except that of being truly and exclusively patriotic
in its sentiment and spirit.

　　　　　" Very respectfully
　　　　　　" Your most obedient servant,
　　　　　　　　　　" JOS. HOPKINSON.
" *Rev. Rufus W. Griswold.*"

It will readily be seen that all party allu-
sions are carefully avoided in the verses; the
fourth stanza, beginning " Behold the chief
who now commands," refers to the President of that time, John Adams, and not to
Washington, as some commentators suppose.

It is scarcely necessary to dwell upon the
faulty rhymes, the exaggerated metaphors;
these were the prevailing faults of the times
when the song was written.

The actor who was to benefit by Mr. Hopkinson's hurried effort was named Gilbert
Fox; he reaped a golden harvest through
the loyalty of his poetic friend.　The Philadelphia morning papers of April 25, 1798,
contained the announcement of Mr. Fox's
benefit, when there was to be performed the

tragedy of "The Italian Monk," [1] — "after which an entire new song (written by a citizen of Philadelphia), to the tune of 'The President's March,' will be sung, accompanied by a full band and a grand chorus."

The success was immediate and emphatic. The theatre was crowded, and the new song redemanded more than half a dozen times. The audience were already familiar with the tune ; before its seventh repetition they had familiarised themselves with the words of the refrain, and finally all stood up and joined with Mr. Fox in the chorus :

> " Firm united let us be,
>   Rallying round our Liberty.
>   As a band of brothers joined
>   Peace and safety we shall find."

The song was soon heard on the streets. In later times the melody which began in company with "The Italian Monk" was

[1] See Preble's "History of the Flag of the United States," p. 716.

continued by the Italian and his monkey; it seemed as if "Hail Columbia" were imperishable.

All national songs undergo some alteration and improvement during their constant usage. Sometimes the original version of such songs is full of musical flaws and harmonic errors. The "Marseillaise" in its early editions had a trumpet fanfare at the end of each verse that would not have passed muster in any musical examination; Carey's original copy of "God Save Great George, our King" had many harmonic errors.[1]   In a similar way, we find "Hail Columbia" in its first version (now in possession of the author) to contain musical progressions that set the teeth on edge.

We reprint this rare and early edition; it will be noticed that the song has not yet received a title, that the combination of

[1] See Chappell's "National English Airs," p. 86, footnote — Doctor Harington's letter.

"Voice, Piano-Forte, Guittar and Clarinett"
is not one which would appeal to any modern orchestral writer, and that the composer
seems to have had one undeviating rule, —
"when in doubt, play the key-note!"

Yet the hearts of the forefathers thrilled
with emotion when liberty was the theme,
and did not greatly mind if its expression
was uncouth. The "Favourite New Federal Song" had come to stay in spite of all
its defects.

Brothers join'd peace and saf-ty we shall find.

2

Immortal Patriots rife once more
Defend your rights — defend your fhore
Let no rude foe with impious hand
Let no rude foe with impious hand
Invade the fhrine where facred lies
Of toil and blood the well earnd prize
While offering peace fincere and juft
In heav'n we place a manly truft ...
That truth and juftice will prevail
And every fcheme of bondage fail
Firm — united &c

3

Sound found the trump of fame
Let Wafhingtons great name
Ring thro the world with loud applaufe,
Ring fhro the world with loud applaufe.
Let every clime to Freedom dear
Liften with a joyful ear —
With equal fkill with godlike pow'r
He governs in the fearful hour
Of horrid war or guides with cafe
The happier times of honeft peace —
Firm — united &c

4

Behold the Chief who now commands
Once more to ferve his Country ftands
The rock on which the ftorm will beat
The rock on which the ftorm will beat
But arm'd in virtue firm and true
His hopes are fixd on heavn and you —
When hope was finking in difmay
When glooms obfcur'd Columbias day
His fteady mind from changes free
Refolved on Death or Liberty —
Firm — united &c

For the FLUTE or VIOLIN

2d time Chorus

CHAPTER VII.

"The Star-spangled Banner" — Its English Origin — Originally a Drinking-song — Doubts Regarding Composer — Its English Uses — A Masonic Ode — Its First American Setting — "Adams and Liberty" — Robert Treat Paine — Its Great Setting by Francis Scott Key — A Doubtful Story Regarding Its First Union with the Music.

WE now come to the national melody which is dearest to the American heart, and, as usual, we find many statements that will not bear the test of investigation, and the customary doubt as to who the composer may have been. Richard Grant White's statement that it is an old French tune has not been substantiated. The earliest form in which we find the melody of "The Star-spangled Banner" is in the guise of an English drinking-song, entitled "To Anacreon in

Heaven." The author is in possession of
an old copy of this, which gives the above
title, and also calls it " A Celebrated Jolly
Song," but presents the name of neither
composer nor author. We give a reprint
of this rare edition after its quaint poem.
The music has been ascribed to Dr. Samuel
Arnold (1739 – 1802), composer to his Ma-
jesty's Chapel, and also to John Stafford
Smith as a transcriber from the " old French
air " aforesaid. The words are attributed to
Ralph Tomlinson, who was, in the last half
of the eighteenth century, president of the
Anacreontic Society of London, a wild bacchanalian club which held its meetings at the
" Crown and Anchor " in the Strand. The
date of the drinking-song may be placed
between 1770 and 1775. Probably at about
the time that liberty had its birth, in
America, the tune which was to become the
chief song of freedom had its inception, in
England.

Here are the verses of the drinking-song :

" To Anacreon in Heaven, where he sat in full Glee,
A few sons of Harmony sent a Petition.
That he their Inspirer and Patron would be;
When this answer arrived from the jolly old Grecian.
'Voice, Fiddle, and Flute,
No longer be mute,
I'll lend you my Name and inspire you to boot.
And besides, I'll instruct you like me to intwine
The Myrtle of Venus with Bacchus's Vine.'
            (Chorus repeats last two lines.)

" The news through Olympus immediately flew;
When Old Thunder pretended to give himself airs.
' If these mortals are suffer'd their schemes to pur-
      sue,
The Devil a Goddess will stay above stairs.
Hark already they cry
In Transports of Joy,
Away to the Sons of Anacreon we'll fly,
And there with good fellows we'll learn to intwine
The Myrtle of Venus with Bacchus's Vine.'
            (Chorus.)

" ' The Yellow-haired God and his nine fusty Maids,
From Helicon's banks will incontinent flee,
Idalia will boast but of tenantless shades,
And the bi-forked Hill a mere Desart will be.

My Thunder, no fear on't
Will soon do its Errand,
And dam'me, I'll swinge the Ringleaders, I war-
rant,
I'll trim the young dogs, for thus daring to twine
The Myrtle of Venus with Bacchus's Vine.'
(Chorus.)

" Apollo rose up and said ' Pr'ythee ne'er quarrell,
Good King of the Gods, with my Vot'ries below ;
Your Thunder is useless,' then, showing his
Laurel,
Cry'd ' Sic Evitabile Fulmen, you know.
Then over each Head
My Laurels I'll spread
So my Sons from your Crackers no Mischief shall
dread.
Whilst snug in their Club Room, they jovially
twine
The Myrtle of Venus with Bacchus's Vine.'
(Chorus.)

" Next Momus got up with his risible Pniz,
And swore with Apollo he'd chearfully join,
' The full tide of Harmony still shall be his,
But the Song, and the Catch, and the Laugh, shall
be mine.
Then Jove be not jealous
Of these honest fellows.'

Cry'd Jove — 'We'll relent, since the Truth you
   now tell us;
And swear by Old Styx that they long shall intwine
The Myrtle of Venus with Bacchus's Vine.'
                    (Chorus.)

" Ye Sons of Anacreon, then join Hand in Hand;
   Preserve Unanimity, Friendship, and Love,
   'Tis yours to support what's so happily plann'd,
   You've the sanction of Gods and the Fiat of Jove.
   While thus we agree
   Our Toast let it be,
   May our Club flourish happy, united and free.
   And long may the Sons of Anacreon intwine
   The Myrtle of Venus and Bacchus's Vine."
                    (Chorus.)

THE ORIGINAL MUSIC.

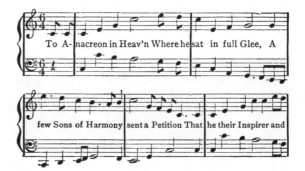

To A-nacreon in Heav'n Where he sat in full Glee, A
few Sons of Harmony sent a Petition That he their Inspirer and

Pa - tron would be, When this An-swer ar - rived from the

jol - ly old Gre - cian,"Voice, Fid - dle,and Flute, no

long - er be mute, I'll lend you my name and in -

spire you to boot; And be - sides I'll in-struct you,like

me, to in - twine The myrtle of Venus with Bacchus's Vine.

CHORUS.

And be - sides I'll instruct you,like me, to in-twine The

And be - sides I'll instruct you,like me, to intwine The

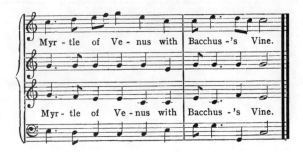

It will be noticed that the music differed in some points, both of melody and harmony, from the present setting.

That the melody was very popular in England is shown by the many editions that were published, and also by the plagiarisms and paraphrases that followed. The author possesses a Masonic setting of the tune which bears the imprint "Dublin, A. L. 5802" (A. D. 1802), which also gives no credit to the original composer. It is contained in "A Selection of Masonic Songs," by Brother S. Holden. We present a fac-simile of this version.

MASONIC ODE.

SONG and CHORUS, Written by M'Connel, on behalf of the Masonic Orphan School. 55

Vivace

To old Hiram, in Heav'n where he sat in full Glee, A few brother Masons sent up a pe-tition, That He, their in-spirer and Pa-tron would be, To help Masons Or-phans, and mend their condition. The Gods were all mute, when he mention'd our suit, They gave their consent, and do-na-tions to boot,

Volti Subito

The Messenger flew, to our Royal Arch Dome,
Where the Masons were seated, in great expectation
The Tyler, was ready; — announced he was come,
When the Lodge was resumed, every Man in his station;
        Our Grand Master there,
            Fill'd the Royal Arch Chair,
When he read, ev'ry Brother with rapture djd stare!
Rejoiced! that the Gods, with donations divine,
To assist Masons Orphans, did cheerfully join.

Strait, the news was made public, the Brotherhood ran,
To announce, to all Masons, old Hirams direction,
They bow'd to the summons, and all to a man,
Clubb'd together their mites, for the Orphans' protection.
    Wives, Widows, and Maids,
    And, Men of all trades,
To ANTLEY s came running to offer their aids,
And, all who contribute donations to join,
For the Orphans' of Masons, are surely divine.

Here, our thanks for each Orphan, is gratefully given,
As you cherish them, may the Gods cherish you,
And, seat you, hereafter, with Angels in Heav'n!
Munificence, never will bid you adieu!
    May free commerce and trade!
    O'er this Island pervade!
And Peace, with her blessings, your happiness aid!
And, long may you live, here, to cheerfully join,
For, Charity purchases blessings divine!

Ye, Brothers, assembled, I now address you,
Prosperity smile on our great institution!
May those whom we cherish, still virtue pursue,
At the shrine of Free-Masonry make retribution,
    May each worthy Brother,
    Protect one another,
And, Secrecy, still shall our Mystery smother;
And, long may Free-Masonry, prudently twine,
Philanthrophy! Charity! Wisdom! and Wine.

We can now examine the American usages of the tune, and it is important to our purpose to show that even in the eighteenth century the melody was known to almost every one in the United States. Its first patriotic setting was made by Robert Treat Paine, in 1798. Mr. Paine seems to have previously devoted his attention to the American employment of English melodies, and in 1794 he had set " Rule Britannia," altering its sentiment into " Rise Columbia." As this was one of the earliest of the patriotic plagiarisms, we append a fac-simile from an edition dated 1798.[1]

[1] " Who wrote ' Rule Britannia ? ' The discussion is raging rather fiercely in Scotland, and it bids fair to be as endless as the question, who composed ' God Save the Queen ? ' Arne, of course, wrote the music of ' Rule Britannia,' but the words of the masque of ' Alfred ' (first performed in 1740 at Clieveden, then the residence of Frederick, Prince of Wales) were attributed jointly to David Mallet, a Perthshire poet, and James Thomson, the poet of ' The Seasons.' No one knows how much each wrote of the six lyrical pieces which the masque originally contained, but Mallet, when he rearranged

RISE COLUMBIA.

An occasional Song written by Mr. THOMAS PAINE of Boston.

When first the Sun o'er O - cean glow'd,

And earth un - - veil'd her virgin breast,

Supreme mid Nature's, mid Nature's vast abode,

Was heard th'Al - migh - ty's dread behest :

Rise Columbia, Columbia brave and free,

Poize the globe and bound the sea.

CHORUS.

Rise Columbia,   Columbia brave and free,

Poize the globe and bound the sea.

In darkness wrapp'd, with fetters chain'd;
    Will ages grope, debas'd and blind,
With blood the human hand be stain'd—
    With tyrant power, the human mind.
        Rise Columbia, &c.

But, lo! acrofs th' Atlantic floods,
    The star-directed pilgrim fails!
See! fell'd by Commerce, float thy woods
    And cloth'd by Ceres, wave thy vales!
        Rise Columbia, &c.

In vain ſhall thrones, in arms combin'd,
  The ſacred rights I gave, oppoſe
In thee th' aſylum of mankind,
  Shall welcome nations find repoſe.
    Riſe COLUMBIA, &c.

Nor yet, though ſkill'd, delight in arms ;
  PEACE and her offspring ARTS, be thine :
The face of freedom ſcarce has charms,
  When, on her cheeks, no dimples ſhine.
    Riſe COLUMBIA, &c.

While Fame, for thee, her wreath entwines,
  To BLESS, thy nobler triumph prove ;
And though the EAGLE haunts thy PINES,
  Beneath thy WILLOWS ſhield the DOVE.
    Riſe COLUMBIA, &c.

When bolts the flame, or whelms the wave,
  Be thine, to rule the wayward hour—
Bid DEATH unbar the watery grave,
  And VULCAN yield to NEPTUNE's pow'r.
    Riſe COLUMBIA, &c.

Rever'd in arms, in peace humane—
  No ſhore, nor realm ſhall bound thy ſway,
While all the virtues own thy reign,
  And ſubject elements obey !
      Riſe COLUMBIA, brave and free,
      Bleſs the Globe, and rule the Sea !

June 1, 1798, the Massachusetts Chari-
table Fire Society celebrated its anniversary
in Boston, with a meeting and banquet.
Robert Treat Paine had been commissioned
to write a song for this occasion. When
first given, it awakened such an enthusiasm
that it was immediately published broadcast.
Paine received $750 for the copyright, an
enormous sum for those days. In the fac-
simile of this work which is given (from the

'Alfred' for Garrick and Mrs. Arne at Drury Lane in
1751, declared that of Thomson's work he only retained
'three or four single speeches and a part of one song,'
and, moreover, inasmuch as he allowed Lord Bolingbroke
to mutilate three stanzas of 'Rule Britannia,' there is
some reason to believe that it was the 'one song' referred
to. For those who know the race best will agree that,
although poets would willingly allow anybody to rewrite
the works of their friends, they would not admit that
even a peer of the realm could improve upon their own
masterpieces. The whole question was thrashed out
when it was raised in 1851 by the late Dr. Dinsdale,
when William Chappell very powerfully urged the claims
of Thomson to the authorship. The Scotch disputants
may meanwhile content themselves with the reflection
that both Thomson and Mallet were born north of the
Tweed." — *London Daily News.*

" American Musical Miscellany," 1798, in possession of the author), it will be seen that the name of the poet is printed as " T. Paine ; " this was, in fact, his name in 1798. He was baptised " Thomas," but when the freethinker of that name began to publish his attacks on the religion of the time, he developed such a dislike of the cognomen that, in 1801, he petitioned the legislature to allow him to assume a *Christian* name, and was graciously permitted to take the celebrated name of his father, one of the signers of the Declaration of Independence, — Robert Treat Paine.

ADAMS and LIBERTY—By T. Paine,

ALLEGRETTO.

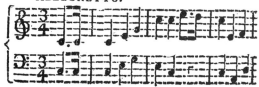

mild   peace, May your   nation in-

creaſe, With the   glory   of Rome. and the

wiſdom of Greece ;   And ne'er may the

ſons   of COLUMBIA be ſlaves, While the

earth bears a plant, or the sea rolls its waves.

In a clime, whose rich vales feed the marts of the
    world,
  Whose shores are unshaken by *Europe's* commotion,
The *Trident* of Commerce should never be hurl'd,
    To incense the *legitimate* powers of the ocean.
      But should *Pirates* invade,
      Though in thunder array'd,
   Let your *cannon* declare the *free charter* of TRADE.

For ne'er shall the sons of Columbia *be slaves.*
While the earth bears a plant, or the sea rolls its waves.

The fame of our arms, of our laws the mild sway,
   Had justly ennobled our nation in story,
Till the dark-clouds of *Faction* obscur'd our young day,
   And envelop'd the sun of American glory.
         But let Traitors be told,
         Who their *Country* have sold,
      And barter'd their *God,* for his image in *gold*—

That ne'er will the sons of Columbia *be slaves,*
While the earth bears a plant, or the sea rolls its waves.

While France her huge limbs bathes recumbent in
   blood,
   And *society's base* threats with wide dissolution ;
May Peace, like the *Dove,* who return'd from the flood,
   Find an *Ark* of abode in our mild Constitution !
         But though Peace is our aim,
         Yet the boon we disclaim,
      If bought by our Sov'reignty, Justice, or Fame.

For ne'er shall the sons of Columbia *be slaves,*
While the earth bears a plant, or the sea rolls its waves.

Tis the fire of the *flint,* each American warms ;
   Let *Rome's* haughty victors beware of *collision !*
Let them bring all the vassals of *Europe* in arms,
   We're a WORLD by ourselves, and disdain a
   division !

While, with patriot pride,
To our LAWS we're allied,
No foe can fubdue us—no faction divide.
For ne'er fhall the fons of COLUMBIA *be flaves,*
While the earth bears a plant, or the fea rolls its waves.

Our mountains are crown'd with imperial Oak,
Whofe roots, like our *Liberties,* ages have nourifh'd
But long ere our nation fubmits to the yoke,
Not a *tree* fhall be left on the field where it flourifh'd.
Should *invafion* impend,
Every *grove* would defcend
From the *hill tops* they fhaded, our *fhores* to defend,
For ne'er fhall the fons of COLUMBIA *be flaves,*
While the earth bears a plant, or the fea rolls its waves.

Let our Patriots deftroy *Anarch's* peftilent *worm,*
Left our Liberty's *growth* fhould be check'd by *corro-*
fion :
Then let clouds thicken round us, we heed not the
ftorm ;
Our realm fears no *fhock,* but the earth's own explo-
fion.
Foes affail us in vain,
Though their FLEETS *bridge* the main,
For our *altars* and *laws* with our lives we'll main-
tain !
And ne'er fhall the fons of COLUMBIA *be flaves,*
While the earth bears a plant, or the fea rolls its waves.

Should the TEMPEST of WAR overſhadow our land,
 Its bolts could ne'er rend FREEDOM's temple aſunder;
For, unmov'd, at its *portal,* would WASHINGTON
  ſtand,
 And repulſe, with his BREAST, *the aſſaults of his* THUN-
  DER !
   His *ſword,* from the ſleep
   Of its *ſcabbard,* would leap,
  And conduct, with its *point,* every *flaſh* to the deep.

For ne'er ſhall the ſons of COLUMBIA *be ſlaves,*
While the earth bears a plant, or the ſea rolls its waves.

Let FAME to the world ſound AMERICA's voice ;
 No INTRIGUE *can her ſons from their* GOVERNMENT
  ſever :
Her PRIDE *is her* ADAMS---*his* LAWS *are her* CHOICE,
 And ſhall flouriſh till LIBERTY *ſlumber forever !*
   Then unite, heart and hand,
   Like *Leonidas'* band,
  And ſwear to the GOD of the ocean and land,

That ne'er ſhall the ſons of COLUMBIA *be ſlaves,*
While the earth bears a plant, or the ſea rolls its waves.

"Adams and Liberty" was, however, not broad enough for a permanent national hymn.[1] It underwent changes enough to prove that all Americans were familiar with the tune of the old English drinking-song. In 1813 it appeared in a Patriotic Songster in Phila-

[1] There is an odd story connected with one of the verses of " Adams and Liberty." In the early days of our Republic it was customary to speak of General Washington in every patriotic poem or song. To give a national hymn without mentioning the Father of his Country was like presenting " Hamlet " without Hamlet. Paine, in his poem, thinking only of the President of that time, Adams, had omitted to introduce the name of the chief national hero. Major Benjamin Russell, of the *Columbian Centinel* (Boston), determined that the omission should be rectified. He, therefore, invited Mr. Paine to a dinner, and when he entered the house caused him to be locked in a room. He shouted over the transom, " You will find pen, ink, and paper on the table," explained the flaw in his song, and told him that he should only come to table after the necessary verse had been completed. Under the spur of this necessity, Mr. Paine wrote the stanza beginning, " Should the Tempest of War overshadow our land ; " a verse not inspired by wine, but by the want of it. This must, however, have occurred before the printing of the poem, for all the early editions to which the author has had access contain the verse in question.

delphia as "Jefferson and Liberty," [1] and on the twenty-fifth of March, in the same year, it was sung at a festival in Boston, "in honour of the Russian achievements over their French invaders," to new words set by Alexander H. Everett.

The above examples may be sufficient to prove that Francis Scott Key must have been absolutely familiar with the melody when he wrote the "Star-spangled Banner." We now approach the creation of the song which, above all others, may claim to be the national hymn of America. In the summer of 1814 the war which was waging between the United States and Great Britain seemed to run almost entirely in favour of the latter nation; Washington had been captured and burned, the shores of Chesapeake Bay were ravaged by the British fleet

[1] Jefferson and Liberty " was set in two ways, first to the tune now used as "The Star-spangled Banner," and, second, to an old Irish air, in 1801.

under Admiral Cockburn, Baltimore itself
was threatened with speedy capture. At just
this juncture, Francis Scott Key, a young
lawyer, determined to seek the British admiral to procure, if possible, the release of
a certain Doctor Beanes, a leading physician
of Upper Marlborough, Md., who was his
personal friend. Procuring proper creden-
tials from President Madison, and proofs that
Doctor Beanes was a non-combatant, Key set
out on his dangerous mission. Cockburn
had transferred Doctor Beanes to the cus-
tody of Vice-Admiral Cochrane, to whom
Key now wended. He could not have come
at a more inopportune moment, for Cockburn had planned a concerted attack by land
and sea, upon Fort McHenry, the key to
Baltimore, at about the time that the American envoy arrived. Vice-Admiral Cochrane
agreed to release Beanes, and treated Key
and his party with considerable courtesy, but
refused to allow them to return just then, as

he feared that the projected attack would be betrayed by the American party, who must have seen the preparations going on in the fleet.   He therefore detained the party on board his son's ship, *The Surprise,*[1] and afterward placed them under guard on their own cartel-vessel during the night of the attack. One can imagine the feelings of a patriotic American, compelled to remain with the enemy during the important battle which ensued.[2]

[1] It is impossible to give some of the details of the detention with historical accuracy. A writer in the *American Historical Record*, January, 1873, says that Key was on the cartel-ship *Minden* when he wrote his immortal song; Col. John L. Warner, in a paper read before the Pennsylvania Historical Society in 1867, says Key "was received with courtesy on board the *Minden*, Admiral Cockburn's flag-ship."   Rear-Admiral Preble, in his excellent "History of the Flag," states, however, that the ship of the line *Minden* was not in the engagement at all and was not one of the fleet at that time.   It was evidently another *Minden* on which Mr. Key wrote his verses, probably his own little cartel-ship.

[2] Mr. Key was at this time a volunteer in the light artillery of Major Peter.

One can also imagine the anxiety with which Key looked toward the fort in the gray of the morning of the fourteenth of September, 1814. The bombardment began at daylight on the thirteenth, and continued throughout the night following. Between fifteen and eighteen hundred shells were thrown, about four hundred falling within the fortifications. Yet only four men were killed, and twenty-four wounded, of the garrison of Fort McHenry. The American party on the cartel-ship had been increased by the presence of Doctor Beanes, whom Vice-Admiral Cochrane had courteously released and given in their charge. The firing suddenly ceased before daybreak of the fourteenth of September. Key and his friend, Mr. J. S. Skinner, who had been one of the party on the *Minden,* walked the deck impatiently, waiting for light that they might see the result. At last they were rewarded by beholding the stars and stripes still floating over the American fort. The three gentle-men were now informed that the attack had failed, that the soldiers were reëm-barking and that as soon as they had got aboard the American party was free to depart.

During the hours of the early morning, beginning with that great moment when he had been able to discern the American flag through his field-glass, Key had hastily jotted down the opening stanzas of the poem, that was to become so celebrated, on the back of a letter which he happened to have in his pocket. He finished it in the boat as he was going up to Baltimore, and wrote out a fair copy at the hotel in that city on the day of his arrival. Copies were immediately struck off in hand-bill form, entitled "The Bombardment of Fort McHenry."

On the twenty-first of September it was printed in the *Baltimore American*, and we we give a reprint of its first appearance in that newspaper :

DEFENCE
OF
FORT M'HENRY.

The annexed song was composed under the following circumstances — A gentleman had left Baltimore, in a flag of truce for the purpose of getting released from the British fleet a friend of his who had been captured at Marlborough — He went as far as the mouth of the Patuxent, and was not permitted to return lest the intended attack on Baltimore should be disclosed. He was therefore brought up the Bay to the mouth of the Patapsco, where the flag vessel[1] was kept under the guns of a frigate, and he was compelled to witness the bombardment of Fort M'Henry, which the Admiral had boasted that he would carry in a few hours, and that the city must fall. He watched the flag at the fort through the whole day with an anxiety that can be better felt than described, until the night prevented him from seeing it. In the night he watched the Bomb Shells, and at early dawn his eye was again greeted by the proudly waving flag of his country.

[1] The cartel, or flag-of-truce boat.

Tune — ANACREON IN HEAVEN.

O! say can you see by the dawn's early
light,
What so proudly we hailed at the twilight's
last gleaming,
Whose broad stripes and bright stars through
the perilous fight,
O'er the ramparts we watch'd, were so gal-
lantly streaming?
And the Rockets' red glare, the Bombs bursting in air,
Gave proof through the night, that our Flag
was still there;
O! say does that star-spangled Banner yet
wave,
O'er the Land of the free, and the home of
the brave?

On the shore dimly seen through the mists of
the deep,
Where the foe's haughty host in dread silence reposes,
What is that which the breeze, o'er the tow-
ering steep,
As it fitfully blows, half conceals, half dis-
closes?
Now it catches the gleam of the morning's
first beam,
In full glory reflected now shines in the stream,

'Tis the star-spangled banner, O! long may
it wave
O'er the land of the free and the home of
the brave.

And where is that band who so vauntingly
swore
That the havoc of war, and the battle's con-
fusion,
A home and a country should leave us no more?
Their blood has washed out their foul foot-
steps' pollution.
No refuge could save the hireling and slave,
From the terror of flight or the gloom of the
grave,
And the star-spangled banner in triumph
doth wave,
O'er the Land of the Free, and the Home
of the Brave.

O! thus be it ever when freemen shall stand,
Between their lov'd homes, and the war's
desolation,
Blest with vict'ry and peace, may the Heav'n
rescued land,
Praise the Power that hath made and pre-
serv'd us a nation!
Then conquer we must, when our cause it is
just,
And this be our motto —'In God is our Trust,'

> And the star-spangled Banner in triumph
> shall wave,
> O'er the Land of the Free, and the Home
> of the Brave.

We have shown definitely that the tune of
the " Star-spangled Banner " was well known
to all patriotic Americans, from 1798 ; we
have shown that it had become customary to
write patriotic poems to the tune ; we have
proved that the *Baltimore American*, which
received the poem almost immediately after
its completion, stated that it was to be sung
to the melody of " Anacreon in Heaven."
We may add that it would be almost a miracle for a poet to write an effusion that should
" accidentally " fit to the involved metre and
irregular form of this melody. Yet no less
a person than Chief Justice Taney, Key's
brother-in-law, and a number of other careless historians, make the statement that
we owe the tune of " The Star-Spangled
Banner " to an actor named Ferdinand

Durang. Here is a detailed statement of this fairy story : [1]

" The tune which has helped so much to make it famous also had an interesting selection. Two brothers, Charles and Ferdinand Durang, were actors at the Holliday Street Theatre in Baltimore, but were also soldiers. A copy of Francis Key's poem came to them in camp; it was read aloud to a company of soldiers, among whom were the Durang brothers. All were inspired by the pathetic eloquence of the song, and Ferdinand Durang at once put his wits to work to find a tune for it. [! ! !] Hunting up a volume of flute music which was in one of the tents, he impatiently whistled snatches of tune after tune, just as they caught his quick eye. One, called ' Anacreon in Heaven ' struck his fancy and riveted his attention. Note after note fell from his puckered lips,[2] until, with a leap and a shout, he exclaimed : ' Boys ! I've hit it ! ' And fitting the tune to the words, there rang out for the first time the song of ' The Star-spangled Banner.' How the men shouted and clapped ! for there never was a wedding

[1] This nonsense is unfortunately repeated in very many quarters, as, for example, Taney's preface to Vol. I. of Key's Songs, Banks's " Immortal Songs of Camp and Field," John T. Ford in *Baltimore American*, etc., etc.

[2] It seems impossible that a musician should need to try over a song which every one in the camp had sung over and over with different words.

of poetry to music made under more inspiring influences." (Gallagher's account, printed in *Harper's Magazine.*)

Never was a bolder or more fantastical claim set up in musical history. Yet Ferdinand Durang deserves at least the credit of being probably the first to sing the song. An account published by the *Baltimore American*, Sept. 12, 1872, contains the following comments on the history of the patriotic hymn :

" The poet, Francis Scott Key, was too modest to announce himself, and it was some time after its appearance [in the *Baltimore American*] that he became known as its author. The song was brought to Baltimore and given to the publishers of the *American*, by John S. Skinner, Esq., who had been appointed by President Madison to conduct negotiations with the British forces relative to the exchange of prisoners. In this way Mr. Skinner chanced to meet Mr. Key on the flag-of-truce boat, obtained from him a copy of his song, and he furnished the manuscript to the *American* after the fight was over. It was at once put in type and published. It was also printed in slips and extensively circulated." [1]

[1] It will be noticed that the account makes a few slight errors regarding Mr. Skinner's meeting with Mr. Key.

In a paper read before the Pennsylvania
Historical Society, in 1867, Col. John L.
Warner thus accurately describes the events
connected with the first singing of the song
to its present melody, by Ferd. Durang :

" ' The Star-spangled Banner ' was first sung when
fresh from the press, in a small one-story frame
house, long occupied as a tavern by the Widow Ber-
ling, next to the Holliday St. Theatre, but then kept
by a Capt. MacCauley, a house where players ' most
did congregate ' to prepare for the daily military
drill, every man being at that time a soldier. There
came also Capt. Benjamin Edes, of the 27th regiment, Captains Long and Warner, of the 39th regiment, and Major Frailey. Warner was a silversmith
of good repute in the neighbourhood. When a number of the young defenders of the monumental city
was assembled, Capts. Edes and Warner called the
group to order to listen to the patriotic song which
Capt. Edes had just struck off at his press. He then
read it aloud to the volunteers assembled, who greeted
each verse with hearty shouts.

" It was suggested that it should be sung ; but who
was there could sing it ? The task was assigned
to Ferdinand Durang, one of the group, and who was
known to be a vocalist. *The old air, ' To Anacreon
in Heaven,' had been adapted to it by the author,* and

Mr. Edes *was desired so to print it* at the top of the ballad. Its solemn melody and expressive notes seem naturally allied to the poetry, and speak emphatically of the musical taste and judgment *of Mr. Key.* Ferdinand Durang mounted an old rush-bottomed chair and sang this admirable song for the first time in our Union, the chorus of each verse being reëchoed by those present with infinite harmony of voices. It was sung several times that morning."

The italics in the sentence are our own. The above is probably a true account of the events connected with the attaching of music to words. That the company could join in the chorus was natural, for the melody chosen was by no means a stranger to any of them, but that Durang first thought of combining the words with their present melody is entirely apocryphal; that honour belongs to Key.[1]

When the origin of the melody of "The

[1] The flag which caused Mr. Key such a frenzy of enthusiasm is still in existence, and a full account of it is given in Preble's "History of the Flag of the United States," p. 732.

Star-spangled Banner " is taken into consideration, many of its defects for choral singing will become self-evident. Its large compass, its constant skipping, the exhilarating upward rush of melody in its opening phrase, its *tour de force* (an old vocal trick, this) in the final phrase, are all admirable adjuncts of a good bacchanalian ditty, but tend to appal the laity in a chorus which calls for great masses of voices. One author [1] has stated that —

" It commences on a key so low that all may join in it. It has unity of idea. The melodic parts most naturally succeed each other, and, if I may so speak, are logically conjoined and bound together. It consists of solo, duett, and chorus, and thus in unity presents variety. It is bold, warlike, and majestic; stirring the profoundest emotions of the soul, and echoing through its deepest chambers something of the prospective grandeur of a mighty Nation tramping toward the loftiest heights of intellectual dominion."

But one may doubt whether the English convivial companions who sang it at the

[1] Elias Nason, " Our National Song," p. 49.

"Crown and Anchor," or the philanthropic Freemasons who warbled it in their lodge-rooms, had even a suspicion of any such emotions concealed in its measures.

Its melody is by no means an ideal one for chorus singing, but its great associations and its lofty words have for ever endeared it to the American heart, and, until some native composer has given us a more practicable tune, "The Star-spangled Banner" will justly remain the national air of our country, and every patriot's breast will throb responsive to its tones.

CHAPTER VIII.

Sea-songs — Charles Dibdin, the Sailor - poet — Sailor Music of America — " The *Constitution* and *Guerrière*," or " Hull's Victory " — A Song of Samoa — " Columbia, the Gem of the Ocean " — Naval Songs of the Civil War.

THE war of 1812 left " The Star-spangled Banner " in its wake, its most important musical result ; but as, with the exception of the defence of Fort McHenry and the battle of New Orleans, the important victories were won upon the seas, it is natural to find much of the music of the epoch consisting of sailor-songs. During the Revolution there had been a few sporadic songs about John Paul Jones,[1] the Scottish hero who had car-

---

[1] " The Yankee Man-of-war," and " Paul Jones's Victory," for example. See " Naval Songs." Wm. A. Pond & Co. Pp. 24 and 48.

ried our flag through fearful combats in European waters. None of these was an American tune, however, and the words were not characteristic enough to be enduring. At about this time England possessed the best sea-songs ever written. The finest sailor-poet of the world was the Englishman, Charles Dibdin, the eighteenth child of a poor silversmith of Southampton, born in 1745, died 1814. Dibdin gave to the British tar an *esprit du corps* that could only have been attained by characteristic themes sung in a manner that the sailors could comprehend. His " Tom Bowling" (written in memory of his elder brother, captain of an East India-man, twenty-nine years his senior, a brother and father in one) remains the noblest picture of an honest sailor in the entire nautical repertoire. Dibdin had the rare faculty, the finest attribute of Burns, of being able to idealise the commonplace. Burns was able to make wonderful poetry even about a

Scottish meat-pudding, — the Haggis, — and sweep from this up to the loftiest declaration of human rights and equality, in —

> " Rank is but the guinea's stamp,
> The man's the gowd, for a' that."

Dibdin, although unable to scale such heights, was entirely adequate to the idealisation of the humble surroundings of sailor-life. What subject could be more humble than a sailor's tobacco-box, with a simple motto scratched on it by his sweetheart ? Yet this became, when gilded by the poet's fancy, the beautiful song, " The Token," with its refrain of —

> " If you loves I as I loves you
> No knife shall cut our loves in two."[1]

The sailor is more constantly at song than the soldier, and it is not surprising to find the sea-songs of both America and England more full of power than the songs of the

[1] The last line is frequently softened into " No pair so happy as we two."

land.   Yet America lags far behind the
mother country in this field.   Dibdin's songs
were so potent an influence in war that, in
1803, the British government engaged him
to write a series of songs, "to keep alive the
national feelings against the French," and
his biographer adds: "His engagement
ceased with the war he thus assisted in
bringing to a glorious close." His songs
were estimated to be worth ten thousand
sailors to the cause of England.

It was not unnatural, therefore, to find
America, during and immediately after the
Revolution, using the songs of Charles
Dibdin; we find them copied in many of the
early music collections on this side of the
Atlantic, during the last two decades of
the eighteenth century.   In the celebration
of the deeds of our naval heroes during the
war of 1812, we still find the custom (most
natural in a nation which possessed scarcely
a single composer) of appropriating foreign

melodies and setting American subjects to them. One example may serve to show the rough but effective character of the entire school, — the song which celebrates the combat between the *Constitution* and the *Guerrière.*

The captains of these two vessels were acquainted with each other and had often bragged of their ships when they met at the London clubs. So strong had this rivalry become that on one occasion a wager of a new hat was made on the result should they ever have a chance to sail against each other. Now, however, the merits of the two vessels were to be tried in grim earnest. Once before the great battle, the two ships had fallen in with each other, off the New England coast.

On the seventeenth of July, 1812, Captain Isaac Hull, in command of the *Constitution,* was sailing northward from Chesapeake Bay, when he fell in with a British vessel which proved to be the *Guerrière,* Captain James

Richard Dacres. Hull beat to quarters and made ready for a fight, but as the morning came on he descried three more war-vessels on the starboard and three more astern, while a seventh soon hove in sight ; he had fallen in with Captain Broke's entire squadron.[1] Thereupon ensued one of the prettiest chases of naval history, lasting sixty-four hours, displaying the perfection of American seamanship, beginning in a dead calm during which Captain Hull was obliged to pull himself forward by a kedge-anchor,[2] gaining somewhat on his pursuers before they discovered the trick. He at last escaped and put into Boston Harbour, determined soon to sally forth and again meet the ship which had given him so much trouble. The opportunity was soon forthcoming. Hull remained awhile in

[1] A number of vessels under one commander, but less than ten, is called a " squadron ; " more than ten is called a " fleet."

[2] A small anchor used for warping a vessel along by casting forward and then hauling up to it.

harbour, carefully training his men in the use of chain and grape shot, and bringing the discipline of his crew to a high degree of perfection.

The *Constitution* did not remain long inactive; Aug. 2, 1812, she set sail to the northeastward, hoping to meet with one of the English war-vessels which now lined the New England coast. Hull especially hoped that he might fall in with the frigate that had caused him to fly during the preceding month. His wish was speedily gratified, although at first it seemed far from fulfilment, for all the way from Boston Harbour to the Bay of Fundy the *Constitution* found no trace of an enemy, the British vessels probably holding a little farther off the shore than Captain Hull's course. After a change of course to the eastward of Nova Scotia and along the Gulf of St. Lawrence, the *Constitution* was put about and turned southward again.

On this course Hull was soon rewarded by the sight of a sail, which proved to be the very frigate he was seeking, and she, too, appeared nothing loath for a fight.   Hull cleared decks for action, beat to quarters, hoisted the American flag, and at once bore down on the enemy, his intention being to come to close quarters immediately.   Dacres hoisted *three* British flags, one at each mast-head.   The old song "Halifax Station" runs :

"Then up to each masthead he straight sent a flag
 Which shows on the ocean a proud British brag;
 But Hull, being pleasant, he sent up but one,
 And told every man to stand true to his gun."

The *Guerrière* had begun firing almost from the moment that the vessels sighted each other; Hull replied with a few shots only, to try the range, and then gave command to cease firing for the time being. A couple of broadsides from the Englishman, given on two tacks, fell short.   Now followed considerable manœuvring to get in a position to deliver a raking broadside. Hull had ordered his men to load carefully with grape.

At last a British shot struck the bulwarks, killing two sailors and wounding several. Lieutenant Morris ran at once to report, but to his eager question, "Shall we return the fire?" Hull replied, calmly, "Not yet, sir." Finally, the *Constitution* was about forty yards to starboard of the *Guerrière*, and in a position to deliver a telling broadside. At once Hull threw aside his calm manner, and yelled, "Now, boys, pour it into them!" That his calmness had been assumed and that his enthusiasm was now unbounded, may be proved by a very odd incident. Hull was a stout man, and he had dressed himself in the fashionable tight breeches of the period; as he shouted his command, he bent twice, almost to the deck, in intense excitement;

when the smoke cleared away, it was seen
that in his energetic antics the captain had
split his beautiful new breeches from waist
to knee; but he did not stop to change
them during the combat which followed.[1]
Another, less humorous sight was afforded,
when the smoke of the broadside lifted;
the deck of the *Guerrière* was strewn with
dead and dying; in a few moments the
mainyard came toppling down, and the mizzenmast soon followed.   "Hurrah, boys,"
shouted Hull, "we've made a brig of her!"
The *Guerrière* brought up in the wind as
the mizzenmast gave way, and the *Constitution* bore slowly ahead, pouring in a tremendous fire, and luffing short around the
bow of the Englishman, to avoid being raked
in return; in doing this, however, she fell
foul of the *Guerrière*, her bowsprit running
into the port quarter of her enemy.

[1] Statement of Lieut. B. V. Hoffman, quoted in Lossing's "Pictorial Field-book of the War of 1812," p. 443.

It was a good chance for boarding parties (except that there was a heavy sea on), but Hull, with his usual prudence, had stationed sharpshooters in the tops of the *Constitution*, and these emphatically discouraged any gatherings of this kind, by shooting down any who seemed disposed to head them. Yankee ingenuity was displayed even in this, for, as in the days of muzzle-loaders it took a considerable time to recharge a gun after firing, the men in the tops lay in clumps of seven, six constantly reloading the discharged weapons, and the best marksman seizing gun after gun, ready to his hand, and making every shot tell.

While the vessels were thus afoul of each other, the forward guns of the *Guerrière* exploded, setting fire to the cabin of the *Constitution*, but the flames were soon controlled.

Now occurred one of the most dare-devil deeds of the whole heroic action ; a stray shot had brought down the American flag, whereupon a young Irishman, named John Hogan, seized it in his teeth, climbed to the masthead amid a shower of bullets, lashed it there, and came down, quite unharmed. Congress afterward awarded him a pension for the bold deed.

One final attempt was made to board, on both sides, and, of the three leaders on the American side, Lieutenant Morris (Hull's second in command) and Master Alwyn were seriously wounded, and Lieutenant Bush, of the marines, killed. Just at this moment the sails of the *Constitution* filled and she pushed ahead clear of her foe, while the mainmast of the *Guerrière* came thundering down, leaving her a hopeless wreck.

The *Constitution* now drew off, knowing that her enemy could not escape, but took a position across the bow of the *Guerrière*, whence she could rake her.[1] Hull's pru-

[1] The battle began a little after 6 P.M., and lasted about forty minutes.

dence was never better displayed than in not forcing a surrender at once. He feared that there might be some consort of the *Guerrière* near by, which might come up, attracted by the firing; he had had one such experience the month before, and he was not in a condition to show a clean pair of heels, as on that occasion. He therefore leisurely took his time to clean up his ship, and only when he was ready to fight another battle, if necessary, with another foe, did he send his third lieutenant, George C. Read (afterward a commodore), to demand the surrender of the *Guerrière*. A jack that had been flying on the stump of the mizzenmast was lowered, but Lieutenant Read desired to make quite sure of matters; he therefore said, "Commodore Hull's compliments, and he wishes to know if you have struck your flag?"

Poor and gallant Dacres! It was a bitter moment to one of the most courageous and chivalric of men; he had been wounded in the contest, and was sore at heart, but he dryly replied, " Well, I don't know; our mizzenmast is gone, our mainmast is gone, and, upon the whole, you may say we *have* struck our flag!" Read then said, "Commodore Hull's compliments, and wishes to know whether you need the assistance of a surgeon or surgeon's mate?" Dacres replied, " Well, I should suppose that you had business enough on board your own ship for all your medical officers!" Read then gasconaded a little. " Oh, no! we have only seven wounded, and they were dressed half an hour ago." [1] He did not mention the seven killed. But against the American loss of seven killed and seven wounded, one must place the British loss of fifteen killed and sixty-three wounded.

[1] This is upon the statement of Capt. Wm. B. Orne. who was a prisoner on the *Guerrière* during the action. Lossing's " Field-book," p. 444.

Dacres then went on board of the *Constitution* and offered his sword to Captain Hull, but the American cried, " No, no ; I'll not take a sword from a man who knows so well how to use it ; but *I'll trouble you for that hat!* " — remembering the wager made in London long before.

It was a battle of which both sides had reason to be proud. Dacres and his men had shown a courage that was so tenacious that, after the battle, it was found that the hull could not be saved, and the *Guerrière*, once called " The Terror of the Sea," was blown up. At the court martial of Captain Dacres, for surrendering his ship, which took place at Halifax a little later, he was unanimously acquitted, and he subsequently became a a vice-admiral, as his father had been before him. In his report of the action, made to Vice-Admiral Sawyer, Sept. 7, 1812, Dacres generously says : " I feel it my duty to state that the conduct of Captain Hull and his officers to our men has been that of a brave enemy, the greatest care being taken to prevent our men from losing the smallest trifle, and the greatest attention being paid to the wounded."

It was customary in those days for the English commanders to send an occasional challenge to the American foe. In this matter, too, Captain Dacres was never very vindictive. Here is a challenge from Sir James Yeo, commanding the English frigate *Southampton :*

"Sir James Yeo presents his compliments to Capt. Porter of the American frigate *Essex*, and would be glad to have a *tête-à-tête* anywhere between the Capes of Delaware and the Havana, where he would have the pleasure to break his own sword over his damned head, and put him down forward in irons."

Not so a man of Dacres's stamp ; he captured Capt. W. B. Orne, of the American brig *Betsy*, and treated him with the greatest courtesy. He sent a challenge to an

American which is in strong contrast with the one quoted above :

"Capt. Dacres, commander of H. B. M. frigate *Guerrière*, of 44 guns, presents his compliments to Commodore Rodgers of the U. S. frigate *President*, and will be very happy to meet him, or any American frigate of equal force to the *President*, off Sandy Hook, for the purpose of having a few minutes *tête-à-tête.*"

It is not necessary to dwell upon the wild enthusiasm which followed the return of the *Constitution* to Boston Harbour. "Old Ironsides," as she was afterward called, in allusion to the strength of her build, was at once celebrated in song and story.

The song which we give in connection with this incident is a fair example of the rough and ready style of its epoch. It is an old English melody called "The Landlady's Daughter of France," and it tells of the battle with a fair amount of detail. It is known to some as "The *Constitution* and *Guerrière*," and to others as "Hull's Victory." It is a "spirited" song in two senses of the word.

CONSTITUTION AND GUERRIÈRE.

It oft times has been told, That the
Brit-ish seamen bold Could flog the tars of
France so neat and han - dy, oh! But they
nev - er found their match, Till the
Yan - kees did them catch; Oh, the
Yankee boys for fighting are the dan-dy, oh!

The Guerrière a frigate bold,
On the foaming ocean rolled,
Commanded by proud Dacres, the grandee, oh!

With as choice a British crew,
As a rammer ever drew,
Could flog the Frenchmen two to one so handy, oh !

When this frigate hove in view,
Says proud Dacres to his crew,
" Come clear the decks for action and be handy, oh !
To the weather gage, boys, get her,"
And to make his men fight better,
Gave them to drink gunpowder mixed with brandy, oh !

Then Dacres loudly cries,
" Make this Yankee ship your prize,
You can in thirty minutes, neat and handy, oh !
Twenty-five's enough I'm sure,
And if you'll do it in a score,
I'll treat you to a double share of brandy, oh ! "

The British shot flew hot,
Which the Yankees answered not,
Till they got within the distance they called handy, oh !
" Now," says Hull unto his crew,
" Boys, let's see what we can do,
If we take this boasting Briton we're the dandy," oh !

The first broadside we pour'd
Carried her mainmast by the board,
Which made this lofty frigate look abandoned, oh !
Then Dacres shook his head,
And to his officers said,
" Lord ! I didn't think those Yankees were so handy," oh !

Our second told so well
That their fore and mizzen fell,
Which dous'd the Royal ensign neat and handy, oh !
"By George," cries he, " we're done,"
And they fired a lee gun,
While the Yankees struck up Yankee Doodle Dandy, oh !

Then Dacres came on board,
To deliver up his sword,
Tho' loth was he to part with it, 'twas handy, oh !
"Oh ! then keep your sword," says Hull,
" For it only makes you dull,
Cheer up, and let us have a little brandy, oh !"

Now, fill your glasses full,
And we'll drink to Captain Hull,
And so merrily we'll push about the brandy, oh !
John Bull may boast his fill,
And the world say what they will,
The Yankee boys for fighting are the dandy, oh !

Other songs of this exciting epoch are
"The *Hornet;* or Victory No. 5," "The
United States and the *Macedonian*," "The
Enterprise and the *Boxer*," etc. They are
all of the uncouth but trenchant character of
the example cited.

Next in chronological order, in the list of
sea-songs of our nation, comes a familiar

song about which there has been, and still is, considerable litigation. It is sometimes called " Columbia, the Gem of the Ocean," and often " The Red, White, and Blue." In an edition published in Baltimore, in 1853, it is called " Columbia, the Land of the Brave." In England it is known as " Britannia, the Pride of the Ocean," and the name of Nelson replaces that of Washington.

Paul Ward, Esq., writes, in " Notes and Queries " of July, 1870:

" When in America I made inquiries regarding the author of this song. My reason for making these inquiries was that, about twenty or twenty-five years ago, I first heard, in 'the Old Country,' this same song sung in our streets, but somewhat varied. The British song sang thus:

" ' Britannia, the Pride of the Ocean,
  The home of the Brave and the Free,
  The shrine of each sailor's devotion,
  What land can compare unto thee! '

It is quite clear that one version must be taken from the other, for each is appropriate only to the eastern or western side of the Atlantic."

Therefore the question arises, has America plagiarised a foreign subject? The author has been unable to trace the melody to its beginning in England, but is assured by several English friends of ripe years that they have been familiar with the melody for about half a century. It is, therefore, possible that the tune is an English one. Nason, in " Our National Song " (p. 55), speaks of it as "set to the English tune of 'The Red, White, and Blue.' "

One cannot lose sight of the fact that "The Gem of the Ocean" is a very odd metaphor to apply to a continent over three thousand miles broad, and bounded by land on two of its sides, and a very apt appellation to bestow upon an island kingdom such as Great Britain is ; and Rear-Admiral Preble points out also that "The Red, White, and Blue" is a misnomer when applied to our flag, for the ranking order of our colours is first, blue (the blue of the union, the firmament of our constellation of stars), then red, and lastly white, — the "Blue, Red, and White," in short, — while Great Britain's flag (spite of the sanguinary name which its sailors bestow upon it), is properly, in ranking order, "The Red, White, and Blue."

But this is not all, nor even the chief controversy, about this hazy song. Many editions give it as the work of "David T. Shaw," but it would seem, at least as regards its American words, to be the production of Thomas à Becket (an Englishman, once resident in Philadelphia), who states his claims and wrongs as follows :[1]

"In the fall of the year 1843, being then engaged as an actor at the Chestnut St. Theatre in this city [Philadelphia], I was waited upon by Mr. D. T. Shaw (then singing at the Chinese Museum) with the request that I would write him a song for his benefit

[1] Letter dated Philadelphia, Dec. 16, 1876, written to Rear-Admiral Preble, quoted in "History of the Flag," p. 755.

night. He produced some patriotic lines, and asked
my opinion of them; I found them ungrammatical,
and so deficient in measure as to be totally unfit to
be adapted to music. We adjourned to the house of
a friend (Mr. R. Harford, Decatur St.), and I there
wrote the two first verses in pencil, and at Miss Harford's piano I composed the melody. On reaching
my home, I added the third verse, wrote the symphonies and arrangements, made a fair copy in *ink*
and gave it to Mr. Shaw, requesting him not to give
or sell a copy. A few weeks afterward I left for
New Orleans, and was much surprised to see a published copy, entitled ' Columbia, the Gem of the
Ocean, *written, composed*, and sung by David T.
Shaw, and *arranged* by T. à Becket, Esq.' On my
return to Philadelphia I waited on Mr. Willig, the
publisher, who told me that he had purchased the
song from Mr. Shaw. I produced the original copy
in pencil, and claimed the copyright, which Mr. Willig
admitted, making some severe remarks upon Shaw's
conduct in the affair. I then made an arrangement
with Mr. T. Osborn, of Third St. above Walnut, to
publish the song in partnership; and within a week
it appeared under its proper title, viz., ' Columbia, the
Gem of the Ocean, written and composed by T. à
Becket, and sung by D. T. Shaw.' Mr. E. L.
Davenport, the eminent actor, sung the song nightly
in London for some weeks; it became very popular
and was published (without authority) by T. Wil-
liams, Cheapside, under the title ' Brittannia, the

Gem,' etc. I visited London in 1847, and found the song claimed as an English composition. (Perhaps it is, I being an Englishman by birth.) During my absence from the land of my adoption, Osborn failed in business, and the plates of my song were sold to Mr. Benteen, of Baltimore. Thus it went out of my possession, much to my regret and loss.

> " I am sir,
> " Respectfully yours, etc.
> " THOS. À BECKET, SR.
" *To Rear-Admiral Preble, U. S. N.*"

It may be added that Messrs. Lee & Walker, of Philadelphia, the successors of the Mr. Willig mentioned above, published a later edition, of which the title-page reads "Columbia, the Gem of the Ocean; *arranged* by T. à Becket, Esq." In one English edition (1866) the song is credited to D. T. Shaw, U. S. A.

Thus "The Red, White, and Blue" follows the example of many national songs in burying its origin in claims and counter-claims. It is sometimes known as the "Army and Navy Song" because it sings

the praises of both branches of the service, and is eminently fitted for occasions where both are celebrating martial
events.

Naturally the Civil War in America
brought forth some additions to the repertoire of sea-songs.   There was heroism
enough displayed on both sides, in naval
encounters, but as the South possessed
but few vessels and scarcely any facilities
for equipping a navy, the preponderance of
naval history belongs to the Union side.
The songs in this field crystallise around the
names of Farragut and Winslow on the one
side, and Semmes on the other.

We present herewith a specimen of the
naval songs of the South.   Its full title
reads "The *Alabama*.   Respectfully dedi-
cated to the gallant Captain Semmes, his
officers and Crew, and to the officers and
seamen of the C. S. Navy, by E. King,
author of the Naval Songs of the South."

THE ALABAMA.

Poetry by E. KING.   Music by F. W. ROSIER.

The wind blows off yon rock-y shore,

Boys! set your sails all free; And

soon the boom-ing can-non's roar Shall

ring out mer-ri-ly. Run up your bunting

taught a peak, And swear, lads, to defend her; 'Gainst

ev-'ry foe, where-e'er we go, Our

mot-to "No Sur-ren-der!"

CHORUS.

ff

Then sling the bowl, drink ev-'ry soul, A

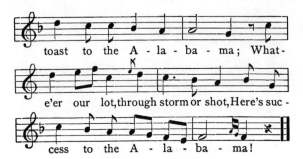

toast   to   the   A - la - ba - ma;   What-
e'er   our   lot, through storm or shot, Here's suc -
cess   to   the   A - la - ba - ma!

Our country calls all hands to arms,
    We hear but to obey;
Nor shall home's most endearing charms
    Steal one weak thought away.
Our saucy craft shall roam the deep,
    We've sworn, lads, to defend her;
Trim, taught and tight, we'll brave the fight,
    Our motto " No Surrender! "
            Then sling the bowl, etc.

Our home is on the mountain wave,
    Our flag floats proudly free ;
No boasting despot, tyrant, knave,
    Shall crush fair Liberty.
Firmly we'll aid her glorious cause,
    We'll die, boys, to defend her ;
We'll brave the foe, where'er we go,
    Our motto " No Surrender! "
            Then sling the bowl, etc.

Boys ! if perchance it may befall,
    When storm of battle raves,

By shot or shell our noble hull
　Shall sink beneath the waves,
Yet while a plank to us is left
　To death we will defend her;
Facing the foe, down, down we'll go,
　But still cry " No Surrender ! "
　　　　　　Then sling the bowl, etc.

There was something of prescience in the last verse, and the subsequent battle between the *Kearsarge* and the *Alabama* was celebrated in more than one song. There is a sailor's ditty regarding this fight, which has something of the bold swing of the music of 1812, the words telling the story in much the same manner that the tale of Hull's victory is related, as a couple of the verses may show.

" It was early Sunday morning in the year of sixty-
　four,
The *Alabama* she steamed out along the French-
　man's shore,
Long time she cruised about, long time she held her
　sway.
But now beneath the Frenchman's shore, she lies off
　Cherbourg Bay.

" A challenge unto Captain Semmes bold Winslow he
　　did send ;
‘ Bring on your *Alabama* and to her we will attend,
For we think your boasting privateer is not so hard
　　to whip,
And we'll show you that the *Kearsarge* is not a mer-
　　chant ship."

In the recent conflict with Spain it was
clearly shown that both sections of the
country, North as well as South, had lost
none of their naval prowess, but the conflict
was too short to give rise to any of that
music which generally follows naval victories.

As a pendant to the above pictures of
martial heroism we may cite an example
of an American deed of generosity and
courage upon the sea, in time of peace.

On Friday, March 15, 1889, the war-
vessels of three nations were gathered together in the harbour of Apia, the capital of
Samoa. England, Germany, and the United
States were inaugurating a protectorate over
the kingdom ; England had sent the *Calliope*

under command of Captain Kane, Germany
the *Adler*, the *Olga*, and the *Eber*, and the
United States was represented by the *Trenton*, the *Nipsic*, and the *Vandalia*. On the
fatal day just mentioned a most fearful hurricane swept down upon the squadrons ; all
the ships were caught upon a lee shore, and,
as their anchors could not hold against the
fury of the tempest, they all seemed doomed
to destruction. The *Eber* soon drove on a
dangerous reef and was a total loss ; the
Adler was on another reef, overturned com-
pletely ; the *Nipsic* had driven ashore and
her men were drowning. Most nobly did the
Samoans labour to save the perishing ; all
accounts of the dreadful event unite in prais-
ing their self-sacrifice and bravery.

Now came the crowning deed of the day ;
the *Trenton* had begun to drag her anchors
and bore down slowly upon the *Calliope ;* in
a few moments the ships would be grind-
ing against each other, and both would be

lost.   The English Captain Kane now determined upon a bold stroke of seamanship ; he
slipped his cable, let his anchors go, and
determined to try and force his way to sea
in the teeth of the hurricane.   It was a
moment of dire suspense ; if the engines
were not powerful enough, the ship with all
on board was lost.   For a moment she went
backward, forced by the elements ; then,
very slowly, inch by inch, foot by foot, but
with gradually increasing speed, the *Calliope*
pushed out to the open sea and safety.   The
American and English vessels were side by
side when Kane's bold effort began, and
when the American sailors saw the *Calliope*
going forth to life, while they felt that they
were doomed to death, they manned the
sides and gave three rousing cheers for the
English captain and crew, and then added
three cheers for the American flag.   It was
the noblest "*Morituri Salutamus*" of history !   One is glad to add, however, that

almost all of these brave men were eventually saved, although there seemed to be not the slightest chance of escape at the time of their cheering the Englishmen.

This noble deed of peace deserves as high a niche in history as the triumphs of war. Thanks to the efforts of an American newspaper, — The *Scranton Truth*,[1] — a song, entitled " The Banner of the Sea," has been written by Homer Greene, and set to music by Fr. H. G. Ganss.   One can cordially reëcho its opening sentiment :

" By wind and wave the sailor brave
　　Has fared to shores of every sea ;

[1] *Scranton Truth* offered a prize, very soon after the news of the event reached the United States, for a poem to fittingly celebrate it.   John Boyle O'Reilly was the judge, and commended the verses of Mr. Greene for the award.   Harrison Millard was the judge of the musical settings and awarded the prize, as above intimated, to the Rev. Fr. H. G. Ganss.   It is seldom that a prize contest brings forth so good a result.   During the Civil War the offer of a large prize for a national hymn was barren of all result.

> But never yet have seamen met
>   Or dared grim Death for victory
> In braver mood than they who died
> On drifting decks in Apia's tide
> While cheering every sailor's pride
>   The banner of the Free."

Spite of the many deeds of bravery which can be credited to the United States Navy, it is only in recent years that our country has taken any rank among the maritime powers of the world. The war with Spain came as a revelation of the strength of a naval force but recently called into being. With the constant growth of this branch of the service, which is bound to follow, we may hope soon to possess a song of the sea that may equal the power of " Rule Britannia."

CHAPTER IX.

Songs of the Civil War — Additions to "The Star-spangled Banner" — The Confederate Flag — "Dixie," and Its Northern Origin — Plagiarisms of War Music — War-song Composers of the North — Prize Offered for a National Hymn — "John Brown's Body" — Julia Ward Howe's Verses — Power of Home-music during the War — Prohibition of Tunes.

AT the beginning of the Civil War, before the song-writers of the North had given many popular songs to the people, "The Star-spangled Banner" was sung with more than ordinary pertinacity and fervour; but it was soon discovered that there was no reference made in that song to any emergency like that which arose in 1861. Many were the efforts to remedy this omission, the best of them being the stanza printed in the *Boston Transcript*, and written by Oliver Wendell Holmes. The added stanza ran as follows:

" When our land is illumined with Liberty's smile,
If a foe from within strike a blow at her glory,
Down, down with the traitor who dares to defile
The Flag of her stars and the page of her story!
    By the millions unchained
    Who their birthright have gained
We will keep her bright blazon for ever unstained.
And the Star-spangled Banner in triumph shall wave
While the land of the Free is the home of the brave."

At the outset the South, too, hoped to use " The Star-spangled Banner " both as her hymn and her flag.   The song had been written by a Southerner,[1] and the flag itself belonged as much to the Southern as to the Northern States.   Some new versions of the famous song were written in the Confederacy, and there were not a few Southerners who desired to claim the United States flag as their own, leaving to the North the task of selecting a new banner.[2]

The committee appointed to consider the

---

[1] Key's descendants, however, refused to sing his song, as belonging to their Northern enemies.

[2] See *North American Review*, November, 1879, p. 486.

subject of a new flag for the Confederate States (Messrs. Miles of South Carolina, Morton of Florida, Shorter of Alabama, Barton of Georgia, Sparrow of Louisiana, and Harris of Mississippi) was not a unit on the matter of discarding the old flag, as witness this excerpt from their report :

"Whatever attachment may be felt, from association, for the Stars and Stripes (an attachment which your committee may be permitted to say they do not *all* share), it is manifest that, in inaugurating a new government, we cannot retain the flag of the government from which we have withdrawn, with any propriety, or without encountering very obvious practical difficulties."

The Confederate general, Wm. C. Wickham, and Admiral Semmes of the *Alabama*, openly confessed regret that the old flag needed to be discarded.[1] Since that dark time, it is good to remember, North and South have shed their blood together for the "Star-spangled Banner."

[1] Preble's "History of the Flag of the United States," p. 508.

But an immediate outcome of the change of flag in the South was the appearance of " The Bonnie Blue Flag," with its spirited refrain :

" We are a band of brothers, and native to the soil,
Fighting for our Liberty, with treasure, blood, and
    toil;
And when our rights were threatened, the cry rose
    near and far
Hurrah for the Bonnie Blue Flag that bears a single
    star.
Hurrah! Hurrah! For Southern rights Hurrah!
Hurrah for the Bonnie Blue Flag, that bears a single
    Star."

But a song was coming that was to become far more typical than this pretty, but not very characteristic, melody ; and the new song of the South had already become popular in the North, where it had its birth.

One cannot set a prosperous counting-house, a busy flour mill, or a number of weaving looms to music ; one can, however, easily reproduce the jovial and romantic plantation life in effective song; and "Dixie" was a rollicking picture of a marked phase of this plantation life. Like "Yankee Doodle," "Dixie" bears its charm in its music rather than in its words. It would seem to be impossible to wed serious poetry to the plantation jingle of its insouciant melody. It has, however, been attempted with both "Yankee Doodle" and "Dixie." The former has received spirited words celebrating Massachusetts (and the gallant stand of her Sixth Regiment in the streets of Baltimore), written by Robert T. S. Lowell, beginning as follows:

> "God bless, God bless the glorious state!
>   Let her have her way to battle!
> She'll go where batteries crash with fate,
>   Or where thick rifles rattle.
> Give her the Right, then let her try
>   And then who can may press her;
> She'll go straight on, or she will die;
>   God bless her, and God bless her!"

And Gen. Albert Pike tried to make
" Dixie " serious with

> " Southrons, hear your country call you !
>   Up, lest worse than Death befall you !
>   To arms ! To arms ! To arms in Dixie !
>   Lo ! all the beacon fires are lighted ;
>   Let all hearts be now united.
>   To arms ! To arms ! To arms in Dixie !
>   Advance the flag of Dixie !
>   Hurrah ! Hurrah !
>   For Dixie's land we take our stand,
>   And live or die for Dixie !
>   To arms ! To arms !
>   And conquer peace for Dixie."

Brilliant and spirited poems both, but
try to sing the first lines only, to the dance-
like themes, and the impossibility of wedding fiery words with jolly music will be
plainly sensed.

" Dixie " was written as a " walk-around,"
by Dan Emmett (born in Ohio in 1815),
and was first sung at Dan Bryant's Min-
strel Show on Broadway, in New York, a
year or two before the war.   The writer of

these lines remembers having heard it when a child as a novelty at these performances. It was one of the war-songs that came into its martial usage by accident.

Musicians may shrug their shoulders as much as they please, great orchestral leaders may state that "Dixie" is "poor music," yet the fact remains that "Dixie" was a great influence on the battle-field, and remains a favourite in days of peace. Abraham Lincoln loved the tune, and many of the Northern soldiers enjoyed its measures even when it represented the enemy to them. It was one of the most characteristic melodies that sprang from the epoch of the war, although written as a picture of peace and happiness. It is thoroughly representative of the "land o' cotton, 'simmon seed, an' sandy bottom," which is more important in such a matter than a severe adherence to the laws of classical form or rigid harmony.

Even as late as the time of the Civil War there was a dearth of composers in America, and plagiarism ran almost as rampant as during the Revolution or the War of 1812. The beautiful German student melody, "O Tannenbaum," was seized upon for "Maryland, My Maryland" and sung to the fiery words of James Ryder Randall. The tune was too good to be lost by either side, and soon after the Southern setting, Northern versions followed, so that the old German praise of friendship and loyalty became a song of war on both sides of Mason and Dixon's line. "When Johnnie comes marching home again" was a near relative of "John Anderson, My Jo," in its opening phrases.[1]

Strenuous efforts were made, at the begin-

[1] Or "Lauriger Horatius."

[2] America has not yet ceased this habit of musical plagiarism. One can find, for example, "Jock o' Hazeldean" turned into "Willie, we have missed you," and the Trio of Chopin's "Funeral March" boldly appropriated for "Somebody's coming when the dewdrops fall."

ning of the war, to produce a hymn that might inspire to patriotism and military ardour. No man has ever yet sat down with the deliberate intention of writing a national hymn, — and produced one! [1]   A national anthem comes by inspiration, and sometimes by accident; sometimes a piece of very worthy music is a failure as national song, sometimes a work which may be strictly classed as trashy becomes a nation's war-cry. In 1861 a number of Northern gentlemen offered a prize of $500, or a medal of the same value, for words and music of a national hymn; May 17, 1861, a committee of thirteen (*absit omen!*) issued the call for this much-wished-for anthem.   There were about twelve hundred competitors; manuscripts poured in from California, from England, from Italy, from everywhere. After filling about five wash-baskets with rejected contri-

[1] The one exception of Joseph Haydn and the Austrian national hymn may again be noted.

butions, the dejected thirteen came to the conclusion that not one of the poets and composers had produced a work that could be called national, or that was likely to become so. The committee reached this depressing conclusion after about three months of hard labour.

That which a public call and a public reward could not evoke, sprang up by accident; an old hymn-tune underwent two or three metamorphoses, and behold, a Union war-song was made! The original hymn-tune is claimed by Mr. William Steffe, a popular Sunday-school composer, as his own.

In one of the old Methodist hymnals of about a half century ago, we find the following hymn-tune with " Glory Hallelujah " words:

SAY, BROTHERS, WILL YOU MEET US.

Say,   broth-ers, will you   meet   us?
Glo - ry, glo - ry, hal - le - lu - jah;

Say,   broth-ers, will you   meet   us?
Glo - ry, glo - ry, hal - le - lu - jah;

Say,   broth - ers will you   meet   us,
Glo - ry, glo - ry, hal - le - lu - jah,

On   Ca - naan's hap - py   shore?
For   ev - er,   ev - er more.

By the grace of God we'll meet you,
By the grace of God we'll meet you,
By the grace of God we'll meet you,
Where parting is no more.

Jesus lives and reigns for ever,
Jesus lives and reigns for ever,
Jesus lives and reigns for ever,
On Canaan's happy shore.

It is a very old camp-meeting song, dating from at least 1856, and is said to have been used in Charleston, both in coloured churches and among the firemen, long before the Civil War. At the outbreak of the war the Second Battalion of Massachusetts's Infantry, familiarly known at that time as "The Tigers," received orders to occupy Fort Warren, in Boston Harbour, and to place it in as good a state of defence as possible. The company possessed a Glee Club, and from this club they had learned the Methodist hymn already given. It was just the kind of rhythmic song that would fit itself to lighten labour with pick and spade and wheelbarrow, and while entrenchments were being thrown up and the rubbish of the old fort carted away, the men sang the swingy tune.

Very soon they began to improvise verses of a less sacred character to the melody. It will be noticed that no rhyming ability was necessary for such improvisations, since the lines are only repetitions of each other. One of the singers in the Glee Club was an honest Scotchman, named John Brown. Many were the jokes that the soldiers used to play on their good-humoured comrade. Finally a jest was made out of the similarity of the soldier's name to that of John Brown of Ossawatomie, and thus the first verse arose, and the song was entitled the "John Brown Song." The words, as printed in the very first edition of this poem (?), were as follows :

"JOHN BROWN SONG!

" John Brown's body lies a-mouldering in the grave,
John Brown's body lies a-mouldering in the grave,
John Brown's body lies a-mouldering in the grave,
His soul's marching on !

CHORUS.

" Glory Hally, Hallelujah ! Glory Hally, Hallelujah !
Glory Hally, Hallelujah !
His soul's marching on !

" He's gone to be a soldier in the army of the Lord,
  He's gone, &c.
  He's gone, &c.
        His soul's marching on!

                CHORUS.

" Glory Hally, Hallelujah! &c.
        His soul's marching on!

" John Brown's knapsack is strapped upon his back —
  John Brown's, &c.
  John Brown's, &c.
        His soul's marching on!

                CHORUS.

" Glory Hally, Hallelujah! &c.
        His soul's marching on!

" His pet lambs will meet him on the way —
  His pet lambs, &c.
  His pet lambs, &c.
        They go marching on!

                CHORUS.

" Glory Hally, Hallelujah! &c.
        They go marching on!

" They will hang Jeff Davis to a tree! [1]
  They will hang, &c.
  They will hang, &c.
        As they march along!

    [1] The " sour apple-tree " evidently came later.

CHORUS.

" Glory Hally, Hallelujah ! &c.
     As they march along !

" Now, three rousing cheers for the Union !
  Now, &c.
  Now, &c.
     As we are marching on !

CHORUS.

" Glory Hally, Hallelujah ! Glory Hally, Hallelujah !
   Glory, Hally, Hallelujah !
    Hip, Hip, Hip, Hip, Hurrah !

" Published at No. 256 Main Street, Charlestown, Mass."

The services of the " Tigers " were not accepted, as an independent battalion, by the government, and many of the men thereupon enlisted in Col. Fletcher Webster's Twelfth Massachusetts Regiment. It was this regiment that bore the song to popularity. Two definite statements from eye-witnesses, in two different cities, will prove this. The present writer has spoken with many people who first heard the tune, and in a manner

which imprinted it for ever in their memory, on Boston Common, when Col. Fletcher
Webster's men marched across it on their
way from Fort Warren to the Providence
depot, to take cars for New York; he has
also the testimony of many who were present, that when the same regiment marched
up Broadway in New York, they halted and
sang the " John Brown Song," and it created
the wildest enthusiasm among the multi-
tude assembled. The Twelfth Massachusetts
Regiment sang it into the war.

It underwent another metamorphosis :
Edna Dean Proctor set abolition words
to the song, in honour of the more celebrated John Brown. In December, 1861,
Mrs. Julia Ward Howe, with her noble hus-
band, the great Doctor Howe, visited Washington. While there she was witness to a
skirmish some miles outside of the city,
and, hearing the soldiers singing " John
Brown's Body," was much impressed by its

effect as a marching song. Rev. Dr. James Freeman Clarke, who was of the party, noticed her enthusiasm, and said, "You ought to write new words to that." Mrs. Howe readily consented to the suggestion, and "Mine eyes have seen the glory of the coming of the Lord," was the result. Therefore the evolution of the chief Northern song of the war can be briefly summed up thus : — A Methodist camp-meeting song, sung in some of the coloured churches of the South, familiar in Charleston, and even made into a firemen's song in that city ; then a camp-song of rather ribald style, carried into fame by the Twelfth Massachusetts Regiment ; then an abolition ode by Edna Dean Proctor ; finally "The Battle-hymn of the Republic," by Julia Ward Howe.[1]

One may add to the above that it was the

[1] To these we must add the mistaken theory of Ritter ("Music in America," p. 439), that the melody was taken from Foster's "Ellen Bayne" (misprinted "Boyne") — a slight and accidental resemblance only.

rhythmic swing of the tune that caused the song to spread so widely and so rapidly; it is one of the best marching-melodies in existence.   It has taken root in England, and it is said that even in the far-away Soudan, General Kitchener's men sometimes made the route less wearisome by singing "John Brown's Body."

There were other songs which served to lighten the soldier's burden on the march, and sustain his bravery in battle, which were written in the North (we have already spoken of the chief music of the South) during the terrible years of strife.   George F. Root contributed the "Battle-cry of Freedom," "Just before the battle, mother," and other strong lyrics ("Tramp, tramp, tramp, the boys are marching," had great success in its time); Henry Clay Work wrote the spirited "Marching through Georgia," and there were many other songs that might be cited, which fitted their purpose, yet fell short of being national music. The influence of some of these songs in time of war can scarcely be over-estimated. There are many songs which in themselves seem simple that acquire a tremendous power by suggesting *home* to the soldier. Thus, for example, there is a simple melody, suggesting to us nothing much more than a few bugle calls, the Swiss "Ranz des Vaches," the call to the cows, that brought such a homesickness upon the Swiss volunteers in the great Napoleon's army, that he was obliged to prohibit it altogether, as it cost him too many troops, the Swiss soldiery deserting when they heard its strains. The Scottish melody, "Farewell to Lochaber," was, in like manner, prohibited during the Sepoy mutiny. A general of the Army of the Potomac recently informed the author that, when the troops were in winter quarters, he forbade playing or singing Charles Carroll Sawyer's famous song, "When this cruel war is over," as it made the men too down-hearted, and "Old Folks at Home" was often under interdict during the Civil War for the same reason.

At the beginning of the war the Southern troops often sang a paraphrase of the " Marseillaise ; " this, however, soon gave way to "The Bonnie Blue Flag," and finally to " Dixie."

CHAPTER X.

Folk-songs — These Also a Branch of National Music — Character of Nations as Reflected in Their Folk-songs — Characteristics of American Folk-songs — Southern Plantation Music — John Howard Paine and "Home, Sweet Home" — Stephen C. Foster — "Old Folks at Home" — Other American Melodies — Music of American Indians.

THE subject of national music can be divided into two large schools. In the preceding chapters we have spoken chiefly of those songs which were calculated to inspire patriotism and martial ardour; but any song of the people, whatever its emotions may be, has a right to be classed as national music, and these folk-songs often give a picture of the nation which evolves them, more graphic than many historic pages.

The folk-song, therefore, spite of its simplicity, has a strength and beauty all its own; it is the wild-brier rose of music, springing up by the wayside of art; seldom can we ascertain who planted it, rarely can we discover how it grew into its final shape, yet, when the greatest composers try to imitate its directness and simple power, they frequently fail.

Sometimes, too, the tender or playful folk-song unaccountably becomes a war-song. In the Crimean War the simple love-song called "Annie Laurie" became the song of every English camp, every British soldier joining in its simple measures:

> "And each one thought a different name
> While all sang 'Annie Laurie.'"

During the Spanish-American War our soldiers, with the usual American devil-may-care spirit, elevated "There'll be a hot time in the old town to-night" into the domain of national music, *pro tempore*, — a quaintly fit selection for the tropics.

The antiquity of the folk-song is remarkable. It is no exaggeration to state that the Bible itself contains many folk-songs of old Palestine, the mourning-song, as it is used to-day, being prominent in Jeremiah, the wedding-song of the Orient appearing in the Song of Solomon, and the favourite vintage-song, abruptly changing into a mourning-song, being clearly perceptible in Chapter V. of Isaiah.

The character of each nation is indelibly stamped on its folk-music, and the folk-song of Russia, in its deep pathos and its bacchanalian wildness, speaks of serfdom, and the temporary escape from sadness, in intoxication ; the folk-songs of Norway and Switzerland resemble each other in the flavour of mountain life which is apparent in them ; the traditional history of England is found in its old folk-ballads ; and the most varied, most ancient, and the most beautiful folk-music of all, the songs of Scotland, speak of every phase of Gaelic and modern Scottish life.

Has America also a folk-song? Certain circumstances have militated against the creation of it. Just as music is often the offspring of sorrow, so prosperity often obliterates the marked types of existence which culminate in folk-song. England's folk-songs meant something while the yeomanry and peasantry were well-defined types; when commercial prosperity made the mother-country one of the most powerful nations of the earth, its folk-song began to decay.

America is handicapped in the production of folk-song both by its business activity and by the fact that it is a gathering of many nations who are not yet amalgamated into a distinct type; at best its folk-songs are sectional rather than national; the life of the West, the South, the North, each presents a different phase which would produce different music, — if it produced any.

But the North (the Eastern and Middle States) is too definitely commercial to reflect romantic life in pathetic music ; the West has not yet developed a singer who can picture ranch life in beautiful tones ; only the South, possessing characteristic surroundings, and a race of natural singers in its coloured population, has developed something akin to an especial folk-song, distinctly different from the music of other nations. A great composer, coming to America from a country which is rich in folk-song (Dvorak, of Bohemia), at once seized upon this music as the most graphic expression of a phase of American life.

It has been objected that the singers in this case are not Americans but Africans, yet we may be sure that though the negroes had remained in Africa a thousand years more, they would not have produced this music ; it is the direct outgrowth of American surroundings, of Southern life. Besides, not all of the singers are negroes ; the note is so definite and clear that many writers and composers, living in the North, have caught its effect and reproduced it with infinite beauty and charm.   Among all these writers one stands preëminent, — Stephen C. Foster. Foster's great-grandfather was Irish, coming to America from Londonderry.   His father, who was a tasteful player upon the violin, lived some time in Virginia and then settled in Pittsburg, and here the best American folk-song writer was born upon a most appropriate date, July 4th, in 1826.   The Southern element which speaks so eloquently from many of his songs, came from his mother (Eliza Clayland Tomlinson), a descendant of one of the oldest Maryland families.   She was a woman of high culture and much poetic attainment.

Foster is said to have much resembled his mother, whom he fairly adored ; in fact his devotion to both his parents was a marked characteristic in this most gentle nature.   He was timid and shrinking in his ways, never in the least self-assertive, and extremely modest. Although educated at Athens (Pa.) Academy and at Jefferson College (Cannonsburg, Pa.), Foster was always a desultory student and was largely self-taught. He made himself familiar with French and German and was a tolerably good painter. He taught himself to play the flageolet at seven years of age. Later on he familiarised himself with the compositions of the German classical composers. He acted as bookkeeper for his brother for some time. His first great success in composition was "Oh! Susannah," and after this he poured out song after song, "My Old Kentucky Home" and "Massa's in de cold, cold ground" proving how thoroughly he was in sympathy with the Southern life and how well he could picture it in tones. He often attended negro camp-meetings and studied the music of the coloured people with assiduity. He married happily, in 1854.

The life which began so charmingly was destined to meet with shipwreck. The appetite for alcoholic stimulant grew strongly upon the young composer; he was unfortunate in business, and this sent him still deeper into dissipation. In 1860 we find him separated from his family, because of his uncontrollable habits, and keeping a little grocery in New York. Pecuniary difficulties caused him to sell his most popular songs for the merest pittance.

His masterpiece must be considered ' The Old Folks at Home" ("Way down upon de Suwannee Ribber"), of which about half a million copies were sold. A more tender lyric of home and its memories has never been written. We pity the musician who finds it "too simple" because it does not stray far from tonic, dominant, and subdominant harmonies; richer musical treatment would, in almost every case, spoil Foster's heart-songs. He died in New York, Jan. 13, 1864, the result of a fall and of gashing himself against a pitcher.

One can only draw the veil of pity over the miserable ending of so sweet a nature; he was, like Burns, a man who sang the purest

poetry of humble life ; may one not carry the parallel further and say of him, as it was said of the Scottish poet :

" The light that led astray was light from Heaven ! "

If " The Old Folks at Home " is one of the chief home-songs of the world, one may also claim its companion work, possibly yet more widely known, as an American produc- tion, but here only the words belong to our country, — the poem of " Home, Sweet Home." John Howard Payne, the author of the words, was born in New York in 1792. He was long in England, was a constant wanderer over the face of the earth, and, after much poverty and neglect, died at Tunis, as United States consul there, in 1852. It is scarcely proper to claim " Home, Sweet Home " as an American song, but we may be permitted to correct a few errors regarding it. It was a song in a musical play entitled " Clari, the Maid of Milan," which Payne wrote in England in 1823. The music was partly composed, partly arranged, by Henry R. Bishop, afterwards Sir Henry Bishop. The play circled around the central point of a song which brings the betrayed and forsaken heroine back to her kindred, — "Home, Sweet Home." In the early printed editions of this work, the tune is distinctly marked "A Sicilian Air," and it is hardly probable that Bishop would not have acknowledged it, had he composed the now world-famous melody. He lived thirty-three years after the performance of "Clari," yet never ,proved his composership of this particular tune, which had meanwhile become celebrated beyond any work that he had written. The play containing the song was first performed at Covent Garden, May 8, 1823, and November 12th of the same year it was first heard in New York, Mrs. Holman being the first to sing the melody in America.

It may be thought necessary, in speaking

of the sources of American folk-music, to inquire whether any debt is due to the Aborigines. The American Indian has never been essentially musical. The subject has been thoroughly investigated by Miss Alice Fletcher, Mr. John C. Fillmore, Mr. H. E. Krehbiel, and Dr. J. Walter Fewkes. To the works of these authorities we refer our reader; as for any direct influence upon American musical art[1] to be exerted by a music that is on the lower savage plane, we have grave doubts; as well expect the Esquimaux, or the Bushmen of Australia, to become the foundation of the opera of the future.

---

[1] Yet Mr. MacDowell has attempted this and brought forth an Indian Suite for orchestra. The Indian, of course, would find his music unrecognisable in this developed state, and a composer of this rank could take almost any unpromising theme or figure and make it of interest to his public. In other words, the Indian themes, unadorned, have no especial inspiration beyond the music of the rest of the savage world.

CHAPTER XI.

IN the opening chapters of this work we
traced the beginnings of psalmody in New
England, regarding that school of music as
the seed whence the greater part of the
American harvest came. Conditions have
changed in recent days, and a worthy school
of American composers has arisen, no longer
copying the Sternhold and Hopkins, or the
Ravenscroft style of composition, but draw-
ing its sustenance from the best German
teaching, and from the influence of the entire
modern school of European music. Yet there

was a connecting link between the ancient psalmody and the modern orchestral and choral composition, in America.

After Billings, Holden, and others of that ilk, there came a set of composers who still leaned toward the music of congregationalism, but added to this a degree of culture and knowledge of the laws of composition which was absent from the works of their American predecessors. Chief among these one can mention Lowell Mason (born at Medfield, Mass., Jan. 8, 1792), whose collections of church music led to a higher taste than would have been possible with the music-books mentioned in Chapter III. His own compositions were simple but well-constructed, and received the commendation of even the great Hauptmann.[1] As a teacher, Lowell Mason had a great influence upon the musical advancement of the country and

[1] Matthews's " Hundred Years of Music in America," p. 42.

might be called the actual father of the modern musical " Convention," the successor of the old "singing-school." He presented a musical library to Yale University,[1] and in many other ways led, along the religious path, to a higher musical development.

With Doctor Mason one may mention Thomas Hastings, Nathaniel D. Gould, Gen. H. K. Oliver, and Geo. J. Webb. These musical reformers had certain tools to work with which the pioneers had not; choral societies and orchestras were beginning to appear in New England, and soon led to similar organisations in other parts of the country.

The most important of the early organisations was the Handel and Haydn Society, which found its chief nucleus in the choir of Park Street Church, Boston, a religious society still existing in its original edifice, at the corner of Park and Tremont Streets.

[1] Ritter's " Music in America," p. 175.

This church was so eminently conservative that it received the graphic nickname of " brimstone corner ; " it at first fought against the wickedness of the use of organs in divine service, using flute, bassoon, and violoncello as a godly substitute for the more varied, and therefore more sinful, instrument. Yet the choir here was by far the best in Boston, and two of its members, Gen. H. K. Oliver (composer of " Federal Street ") and Mr. Jonas Chickering (founder of the piano house of Chickering & Sons), were destined to exert a marked influence upon the American musical world, a little later. Out of this choir came the Handel and Haydn Society.

There had been a Peace Jubilee held in King's Chapel, to celebrate the end of the War of 1812, on the night of Feb. 22 (Washington's birthday), 1815, and Boston was so delighted with the choral music on that occasion, that the papers suggested more effort in the same line. The result was that on March 30, 1815, a circular was sent out by Gottlieb Graupner, Asa Peabody, and T. S. Webb, inviting coöperation, "for the purpose of forming a correct taste in Sacred Musick."[1] This circular led to the immediate birth of the Handel and Haydn Society. The constitution of the new society followed on April 20, 1815, and Christmas eve, of the same year, brought forth its first concert. General Oliver has personally told the author that it was the most impressive of concerts, the composer of "Federal Street" having been one of the auditors. The programme was a very ambitious one for those days ; it began with seventeen numbers (recitatives, airs, and choruses) from Haydn's "Creation." Then came a number of Handelian selections, and as finale the "Hallelujah Chorus"

---

[1] There had been a musical society established earlier than this, in Stoughton, Mass., Nov. 7, 1786. But the Stoughton Musical Society never exerted the influence of the Handel and Haydn, although it may claim chronological precedence.

was sung. The tickets were one dollar each, but the advertisement in the Boston *Columbian Centinel* added :

" N. B. Gentlemen who wish to take their families are informed that on purchasing *four* tickets they will be presented with a *fifth* gratis ; and those purchasing *six* will be entitled to *two* additional ones."

The concert began at six o'clock, and, like the Peace Jubilee, was held in the " Stone Chapel in School Street " (King's Chapel) ; it must have lasted until about ten o'clock or later. There were ninety gentlemen and ten ladies in the chorus, there was an orchestra of ten, and the organ. There were 945 people in the audience.

Criticism in those days was largely ecstasy,[1] and the raptures of the press are comical to behold : " There is nothing to compare with

[1] One may regard the late John S. Dwight as the link between the old criticism and the new, exactly as Lowell Mason leads from the old style of composition to the more advanced modern school ; both deserve the gratitude of American musicians.

it ; it is the wonder of the nation," exclaimed
one reviewer ; here is an extract from the
Columbian Centinel of Dec. 27, 1815 :

> " We have not language to do justice to the feel-
> ings experienced in attending to the inimitable execu-
> tion of a most judicious selection of Pieces from the
> Fathers of Sacred Song. We can say that those who
> were judges of the performances were unanimous in
> the declaration of their superiority to any ever before
> given in this town.   Some of the parts electrified the
> whole auditory, and notwithstanding the sanctity of
> the place and day, the excitements to loud applause
> were frequently irresistible.   We shall not particu-
> larise, but some of the solos merited every praise."

In 1818 the Handel and Haydn Society
gave the first complete performance of an
oratorio that had ever taken place on American soil,[1] presenting the " Messiah," which it
has since sung about one hundred times.
In 1819 it gave a complete performance of

---

[1] Ritter's statement ("Music in America," p. 135) regarding a performance of the " Messiah " in New York, at
Trinity Church, in 1770, is not exact ; a partial performance was given.   Dr. Ritter contradicts his own statement
on page 229 of the same work.

Haydn's " Creation." New York was several
years behind Boston in this field, the " Sacred
Music Society " giving the first entire oratorio in that city — " The Messiah " — Nov.
18, 1831. The Handel and Haydn Society
soon left the Stone Chapel, and its concerts took place at Boylston Hall (corner
of Boylston and Washington Streets), then
at the Melodeon (on Washington Street,
between West and Avery Streets), and finally
at Music Hall. Until 1847 the president of
the society was also its conductor, and in the
old list we find the names of Thos. S. Webb
and Lowell Mason, followed by Zeuner,
Charles C. Perkins, Carl Bergmann, and culminating in the directorship of Carl Zerrahn,
extending over forty years. Like Mason in
sacred music, or Dwight in criticism, Carl
Zerrahn was the bridge by which New England, and afterward the rest of the United
States, travelled to its modern goal in classical music.

The list of the organists presents Miss Hewitt (afterward Mrs. Ostinelli), the two Hayters, Mr. J. C. D. Parker, reaching its culmination in the work of B. J. Lang, who served about forty years, and whose name is also intertwined most closely with almost every advance made in New England, from the crude performances of the past, to the advanced taste and virtuosity of the present. It may also be mentioned that Lowell Mason published a collection of the best oratorio music, as an outgrowth of the work of this society, called the " Handel and Haydn Collection," a book which might fairly be called "epoch-making," so distinctly does it mark the advance of American musical taste.

New York was far behind Boston in the choral side of music, for its first important choral society, " The Musical Institute," was established as late as 1844, and even this society was short lived, being merged in the New York Harmonic Society in 1849, this latter being New York's first great choral society. The taste for oratorios was not nearly so universal in New York as in Boston.[1]

Contemporaneous with these advances in choral performance the western and southern cities were influenced by foreign causes; the German population instituted many male choruses (*Maennerchoere*), and the opera was accepted with some avidity by cities outside of New England. It is not to our purpose to follow the establishment of Italian and French opera in the United States, yet the following facts may present a summary of matters.

New York was the pioneer. In 1825 an effort was made to establish Italian opera in that city. The era of high salaries began at once, America surpassing England in the extravagance of its remuneration of foreign artists. Henry T. Finck, in an interesting article on this subject, states that the price

[1] Ritter's " Music in America," p. 296.

of a good orchestra seat in that first great season of opera in America was one dollar ! [1]

This first cis-Atlantic opera troupe was brought to New York by the great Manuel Garcia. [2] From that time to the present, Boston has been but a reflection of New York in operatic matters. In the earliest days of the history of opera in America, Boston looked askance at such " play-house " affairs. When the Marti troupe came to Boston (at the Howard Athenæum) in 1847, the prices were less than those exacted in New York, fifty cents paying for admission even when Madame Lagrange sang. At this time New York loved opera, and was bored by oratorio, while Boston cared less for Rossini or Mozart than for Handel and Haydn. This was a natural outgrowth of the old psalmody in which New England had been bred, and

[1] *The Musician*, December, 1897.

[2] A full description of the evolution of opera in America will be found in Ritter's " Music in America," p. 190 *et seq.*

was also a consequence of the early establishment of choral and orchestral music in the eastern, and opera in the central, metropolis. We have outlined the native choral development; let us now turn to a brief sketch of the rise of the orchestra in America.

In this field Boston was again the pioneer. Philadelphia, in the last century, was very musical, and as early as May 4, 1788, gave, at the Reformed German Church, in Race Street, a concert with a chorus of two hundred and thirty, and an orchestra of fifty members; the greatest musical event of the last century, in America. Yet even Philadelphia made no effort to establish an orchestra upon anything like a permanent basis.

In 1798 there came to Boston a man who may well be called the father of the American orchestra; his name was Gottlieb Graupner. He had been the oboist in a Hanoverian regiment in his youthful days, and after his discharge from service became

a rolling stone, which only began to gather
moss when it brought up in Boston.   He left
his regiment April 8, 1788, and in 1791
we find him in London, playing oboe in the
great orchestra which Salomon gathered to
give Haydn's symphonies, under the personal
direction of the composer.   We next en-
counter our strolling musician in Prince
Edward Island, where he must have found
very little chance to exercise his talents, for
he soon set sail for Charleston, S. C., where
he married and remained a few years.   His
wife was also a good musician and a talented
singer.   In 1798 the wanderings ended, and
our musician settled in Boston, where there
were then about half a dozen professional
musicians.   He very soon drew these, and
a few amateurs, around him.   He was the
very man to head a country orchestra, such
as was now to be founded, for he not only
played his oboe, but was a good performer
upon the double-bass, could sustain an or-

chestral part on the clarinet, played piano, and was an excellent timist. In addition to this general utility work he was a music teacher, a music engraver, and opened a musical warehouse in Boston.

He very soon had his little orchestra in working order, beginning with about ten members. The rehearsals were held in Pythian Hall in Pond Street (now Bedford Street), and the band played at Gyrowetz's symphonies (almost unknown nowadays), and finally scaled the heights of Haydn, whom Graupner always idolised. In 1810 the little orchestra was named the "Philo-harmonic," and at once combined with the choral performances of the town. It coöp-erated with Dr. G. K. Jackson, the organist of King's Chapel, and at the early meetings of the Handel and Haydn Society we find the members of the Philo-harmonic Society invited as co-workers. The Dr. G. K. Jackson mentioned above was also an important figure in the advancement of instrumental as well as choral music. He was an Englishman, and came to Boston in 1812, becoming organist in the chief churches here, and the most prominent music teacher in the town; he was rather haughty toward the incipient efforts of the American choral societies, and held aloof from the Philo-harmonic and the Handel and Haydn societies, until they were thoroughly established without his aid.

In 1833 came the next important advance. Lowell Mason was now active in Boston's music, and, with the assistance of Hon. S. A. Eliot, Mr. Webb, and other music-lovers, the "Academy of Music" was founded. This was practically a musical conservatory; it intended not only to give instruction in all branches of music, but to establish lectures, concerts, choruses, to elevate church and school music, to publish musical essays, etc.

No musical institution in America at that

time could carry out such a stupendous programme, but the academy taught twenty-two
hundred pupils in the first two years, a very
good proof of the public interest in music in
New England. In 1837 the academy founded
an orchestra, but it now found that it was
going too far in its schemes to retain full
pecuniary support from the public. It nevertheless struggled on until 1847, when it gave
up the ghost. It had done much in the general
field of music ; at one time it was recognised
as the chief authority of the country in this
branch of art, and letters from almost every
State in the Union, to " The Academy of
Music," prove that Boston was a musical
centre even in the first half of the nineteenth
century. But the greatest good in connection with the academy was the impetus which
such of its promoters as George J. Webb,
William C. Woodbridge, and Lowell Mason
gave to the teaching of music in the public
schools. The planting of this seed was one of

the greatest factors in the musical advancement of America.

From 1841 the academy devoted itself more exclusively to instrumental music, and through its efforts Boston received its first large orchestra, an organisation which lasted during the last seven years of the existence of the academy.   The Musical Fund Society carried on intermittent, light orchestral concerts until 1855, under Tom Comer's (no one ever called him "Thomas" Comer) direction. Mr. Comer was succeeded by Mr. George J. Webb, who gave some very ambitious programmes.

But now a foreign yeast was in the meal and the orchestral music of America began to draw inspiration from the fount of Germany. The year 1848 was a very trying epoch for the fine arts in Europe ; revolution was lifting its head on every side ; thrones were tottering and dynasties crumbling ; freedom was in the air in almost every monarchy of the old world. Naturally concerts languished because of the political excitement. Musicians began to emigrate to England and to America, the only two countries which remained calm and prosperous amid the storm.

It was at this time that a number of young musicians came to New York and organised themselves into an orchestra. In 1848 they took the name of "The Germania Orchestra," made Boston their headquarters, and had Carl Lenschow as the first conductor. In 1850 the orchestra consisted of twenty-three musicians, with Carl Bergmann at its head. Among the band was a tall young flute-player, named Carl Zerrahn, who subsequently was made director. This orchestra may be called the first organisation which gave satisfactory performances of the great symphonies in America. The orchestra soon grew to fifty members and even the greatest works, Beethoven's ninth symphony for example, were interpreted. The Germania dissolved in 1854; in five seasons it had given nearly ninety concerts in Boston and had made a succession of tours to New York and to other cities, giving Americans the first true model of orchestral work in the classical forms.

It will be impossible, in a volume not exclusively devoted to the subject, to speak of all the musical societies, orchestras, choral societies, etc., that were now in existence, and those which afterward sprang into being : let us rather trace the orchestral seed which was planted in Boston, the chief orchestral city of the United States, to its perfect fruit.

After the Academy of Music the influence of the Harvard Musical Association was an important factor in the advancement of orchestral matters. This association sprang, in 1837, from the Pierian Sodality. It devoted itself to advancing music in every form. At first it founded a musical library, then gave glee club concerts, then introduced chamber concerts, supporting the Mendelssohn Quintette Club in its early, classical career; in 1851 it agitated the subject of a Music Hall for Boston, and the edifice was opened Nov. 20, 1852, the Handel and Haydn Society and the Musical Fund Orchestra giving the first concert.

From 1854 to 1866 there had been considerable irregularity in the orchestral music of Boston, although from 1855 to 1863 a Philharmonic Orchestra under Carl Zerrahn existed. The taste of the country in the symphonic field was of the flimsiest description. An indisputable proof that Boston was the leader in orchestral taste even at this epoch, may be found in tracing the early efforts of the Germania Orchestra mentioned above. In New York the Germania musicians met with a pecuniary loss; in Philadelphia they started at Musical Fund Hall and lost so much that they went to the Chinese

Museum (a much smaller edifice), and this also proving too large, they finally were obliged to try a little room in Arch Street, which they hired for ten dollars; but the receipts amounted to only nine dollars and a half, so the landlord extinguished the gas and the concerts simultaneously! Only in Boston did the organisation receive due encouragement and sufficient support to continue its venture.

Yet even Boston, from 1863 (when Mr. Zerrahn discontinued his Philharmonic concerts) to 1866, had an interregnum in its orchestral music. In 1866 the Harvard Musical Association took up the task of providing symphonic concerts for the city; Mr. Zerrahn was placed at the head, and until 1882 the concerts were given by the Harvard orchestra.

But at this time Boston suddenly began to burst its classical swaddling clothes! The city now boasted plenty of musicians of European culture, and these began to demand a more modern style of programme than the selections from the old masters which were copiously in evidence in the Harvard programmes, and it was suggested, also, that the German style of orchestral ensemble had by no means been attained. The result was that Boston suddenly had *two* regular orchestras, the Philharmonic Orchestra (a name three times used in Boston's musical history) beginning independently in 1879, and organising into a Philharmonic Society in 1880. The conductorship of this orchestra was held successively by Bernhard Listemann, Louis Maas, and Carl Zerrahn. Orchestral matters were seething in Boston at this time ; every music-lover was seized and questioned, — "Under which king, Bezonian ? Speak or die ! "

The Harvard Musical Association represented musical conservatism, the Philharmonic Society was identified with radicalism of the most decided type. One may well acknowledge the great services of both societies, yet we need not close our eyes to the inevitable shortcomings that necessarily were present in the performances of each. With the comparatively slight patronage that was then given to symphonic concerts, both organisations were likely to be conducted at a pecuniary loss. In order to make this deficit as light as possible (there was scarcely a hope of avoiding it altogether), the rehearsals were few and far between, and the musicians, gaining their chief livelihood by teaching, by playing at parades and picnics, or by theatrical work, could not give more than a perfunctory attention to the symphonic task. It was necessary to build up an orchestra which should offer permanent and continuous employment to its members; an orchestra that should allow the player to devote his best energies to the highest branch of his work, without incurring the risk of starvation. But

what society would undertake this reconcilia-
tion of art and bread-and-butter? Would the
government grant a subvention after the
manner of Europe? Only a public-spirited
man of great wealth could, by jeopardising
part of his fortune, accomplish the devoutly-
wished-for consummation. The man came;
Henry L. Higginson, a prominent Boston
banker, offered to found the ideal orchestra for Boston, a model too for the entire
country.

Few can understand what such an under-
taking meant; there was not only the almost
certain deficit which would need to be made
good during the first years of the enterprise,
but there were sure to be a host of annoy-
ances in ruling the new body, in bringing it
into shape; cares and worries from which
any man might well shrink.

CHAPTER XII.

IN approaching the end of our subject, a
retrospect may well be allowed; beginning
with square-cut psalmody, with a proscrip-
tion of secular music, with a most primitive
orchestra, in a little more than a century
America has become, at least in its chief
cities, a field for the best music that the
world can afford, and if the public taste is
not yet on a par with the culture of European art-centres, at least there have been giant
strides toward that desideratum. This has
been chiefly due to four causes: the advances

made in the standard of musical performances, the creation of a splendid band of
native composers, the establishment of great
and thoroughly equipped music schools and
conservatories, and the evolution of a good
system of public-school training in vocal
music.

It is not to our purpose to speak in detail
of all these branches; W. S. B. Matthews
and F. L. Ritter have told the story of the
American composer; the history of American public-school music demands a volume to
itself. It may be stated, however, that two
cities have led the way toward the high
standard of public performance now attained
in this country. Boston, which once led in
the matter of vocal performance, has had the
leadership wrested from her by New York.
Among all musical forms those which com-
bine vocal and instrumental forces may be
considered the highest, and, as oratorio offers
a scant field both in the matter of com-

posers and of public appreciation, the opera may well be acknowledged the chief and most important of all musical forms.

In this direction New York, even from the early part of the nineteenth century, has been the acknowledged guide of the entire country, her achievements culminating with the highest type of German operatic performance under the leadership of the great Anton Seidl. Nor was the metropolis without its own musical societies in the days of America's infancy, although these came somewhat later than the New England choral and orchestral organisations described in the preceding chapter. As early as 1770, Trinity Church gave partial performances of " The Messiah ; " in 1824 there existed a New York Choral Society which gave solid classical programmes, and in 1831 the Sacred Music Society gave the first entire performance of an oratorio, but the public taste for the earnest side of composition was not, at that time, so developed as in Boston. Trumpet and trombone playing was more appreciated than good singing or the finer points of music.

Shortly after 1830 we find the Musical Fund Society, the Euterpean Society, and the Sacred Music Society coëxistent in New York. The Euterpean Society was an instrumental one and had been in existence from the very beginning of the nineteenth century, being founded a trifle later than Graupner's little band in Boston.

But the real beginning of thorough musical organisation took place at a much later time. The New York Philharmonic Society first organised April 2, 1842, and gave its opening concert Dec. 7, 1842. This association, so important in the development of orchestral music in this country, was mainly due to the efforts of Uriah C. Hill, a native New Yorker, who had studied abroad and desired to found a society like the London Philharmonic, for the study and performance of the great symphonic works. After some years of effort the organisation grew to good dimensions and was incorporated Feb. 17, 1853. Many societies in every field of music have been incorporated since that time, but none has been such an important factor in New York's orchestral history as the Philharmonic Society.[1]

The highest orchestral standard, however, which America ever attained, has been achieved by the Boston Symphony Orchestra, an organisation which may well compare with any of the orchestras of Europe. We have already, at the end of the preceding chapter, sketched the circumstances which led to the establishment of this band. It began its labours in 1881. In order not to antagonise the orchestras then existing in

[1] It would be impossible to speak of all the modern musical societies of New York and Boston, but the Oratorio Society of New York, established by Dr. Leopold Damrosch in 1873, deserves mention as among the most important of these.

Boston, its generous founder, Mr. Henry L. Higginson, took the off-night of the week for his concerts. The old Puritans considered Saturday night as the beginning of the Sabbath ; long after this religious idea had passed away, Boston still held Saturday night sacred as regards theatre or public performances ; up to the last quarter of the nineteenth century the oldest theatre of the city, the Boston Museum, closed its doors on Saturday night. It was this unused night which the Symphony Orchestra chose for its concerts, and Saturday, Oct. 22, 1881, the Boston Symphony concerts were begun.[1]

In accordance with the plan introduced to America by the New York Philharmonic Orchestra, each concert was preceded by a public rehearsal, thus giving the ardent

[1] See articles on this subject by the author in *The Musician* for December, 1897, and *New England Magazine,* November, 1889.

musical student an opportunity of hearing any new or important work twice in close repetition, if desired.   Mr. George Henschel was the first conductor.   Great as this artist was in the other domains of music, he had not yet won his spurs as an orchestral conductor, therefore a new conductor and a new orchestra were launched simultaneously.

Certain odd experiments were made in the placing of the men during the first season ; all of the string departments were divided into two sections, sitting on each side of the conductor, save one lonely bass-fiddler who could not be divided, and stood at the rear, alone, like James's " solitary horseman." This arrangement was subsequently abandoned, and the ordinary seating adopted.

There were sixty-seven members of the orchestra at first, many of them old residents of the city, and most of them members of the two orchestras already described. Twenty concerts were given the first season ;

the third season this was increased to twenty-
six (always with an equal number of public
rehearsals), and then the number settled
down to twenty-four, which has been the
regular number annually ever since.

From the very first, because of the adequate number of rehearsals, the performances
went beyond anything that Boston ever possessed save in the occasional concerts of
Theodore Thomas's excellently drilled travelling orchestra, and as the years rolled by
the standard went far beyond anything that
was anticipated at the beginning. In order
to make the programmes thoroughly educa-
tional, Beethoven's nine symphonies formed
the backbone of each of the early seasons,
until every music-lover in Boston knew them
almost by heart. Mr. Henschel had also a
habit of "saying grace" in a musical manner
by beginning every season with Beethoven's
"Dedication of the House" overture.

Another reform was necessary before the

ideal of orchestral performance could be attained ; in the ranks there were many old
musicians who had passed the zenith of
their powers, but were kept on for sentimental reasons ; these needed to be replaced
by stronger performers, young men if possible, who should grow up with the orchestra, and make future changes unnecessary
for many years to come. A new conductor
began the fourth season, and set about this
necessary but very ungracious task, — Mr.
William Gericke. His work began Oct.
18, 1884, and was an excellent example of
the "suaviter in modo, fortiter in re" principle, the hand of iron in the glove of
velvet. Great was the indignation when
the new broom began to sweep ! Especially
harsh seemed the replacing of the great
violinist, the musical pioneer, the leader of
the orchestra (concert-meister), — Bernhard
Listemann, — by a beardless young Rouman-
ian. After the lapse of years, one can see

that the change was not a deterioration, for
the young man has since become one of
the foremost of our musicians, the founder
of a great string quartette, and one of the
best of concert-meisters, — Franz Kneisel.
But when the youthful newcomer, on Oct.
31, 1886, came before the Boston public as
a soloist for the first time, it was decidedly a
case of Daniel in the lion's den, — and the
latter-day Daniel escaped unscathed also.

The change was a typical one, for Mr.
Gericke brought a number of young musicians into the Boston Symphony ranks who
have been there ever since, with the result
that there have been few changes in the
personnel of the orchestra for the last dozen
years. When it is borne in mind that the
number of public performances of the Boston Symphony Orchestra in Boston, New
York, and Philadelphia, and other cities,
reaches very near the one thousand mark
in 1900, that the same body of men have

rehearsed together *thousands* of times, it will be seen that the Boston Symphony Orchestra (now consisting of about ninety members) has had advantages possessed by no other instrumental organisation that America has ever owned, and its unrivalled technical excellence will readily be understood.

In 1889 Mr. Gericke voluntarily left his post, his health necessitating a return to Europe.   The homage which Boston paid to him at his departure can scarcely be exaggerated.   It is not necessary to speak of each conductor in detail; we find the great orchestral virtuoso, Mr. Arthur Nikisch, in control from 1889 to 1893; in 1893 the broad-minded and thoroughly equipped Emil Paur was the conductor, and remained so until he left for orchestral and operatic work in New York in 1898; in 1898 Mr. Gericke again took charge of the orchestra which he had done so much to establish.

One cannot repress the wish that this

great orchestra may some day go to Europe, that the Old World may be taught to realise what a standard of musical interpretation has been attained in America.

Nor is this orchestra the only one to which our country may point with pride. Theodore Thomas (born in Hanover, Germany, in 1835), who had been giving symphonic concerts in New York, at Irving Hall first, then at Terrace Garden (1866), and finally at Central Park Garden (1868), eventually organised a travelling orchestra, and taught all America the classical as well as the most modern repertoire of orchestral music. Probably no foreigner ever exerted such a widespread influence on the national musical taste in America, in modern days, as Theodore Thomas. After being director in numerous festivals, and conductor of hundreds of concerts in almost every State of the Union, he was, in 1890, appointed conductor of a permanent orchestra in

Chicago, and his influence there has been very beneficent. At the World's Fair in Chicago, the work of this classical musician was apparent in every orchestral detail.

With the World's Fair of 1893, we come to the paths of strictly national music again, for the committee of that mighty festival appealed to the great American composers to furnish new selections that should be national music. The result was again a proof that such music is not made to order, for, although our greatest composers were heard from, nothing that can by any stretch of fancy be called permanent, resulted. A similar result attended the effort to bring national music out of the Centennial Exposition at Philadelphia, in 1876, a most bombastic march by the great Wagner, which was composed for the occasion, being about as national as a performance of "Rienzi" would have been.

A festival which took place before either

of the two above-mentioned, was more fortunate in its evolution of a song which came
near to being national.

During the Civil War there lived in Boston
a German composer named Matthias Keller;
he was a kind, simple, and lovable old man,
who struggled along in poverty, trying his
hand at all the smaller forms of composition,
and failing to attract the attention of the
public in any of them. In common with all
the composers of that time he evolved a war-
song; it was called "Save our republic, oh,
Father on high," and it resembled a chorale
rather than a military work. It attracted
temporary notice and then fell out of sight.

Patrick Sarsfield Gilmore, a very enter-
prising Irishman, — not too heavily burdened
with classical tastes, — in 1869 gave a festival
in Boston, celebrating the close of the war.
It was a very different affair from that with
which, in 1815, Boston had celebrated the end
of the War of 1812; ten thousand singers in

the chorus, eight hundred musicians in the orchestra, proved that Gilmore disdained the retail business in music.   There are always plenty of people who figure music upon arithmetical principles, *i. e.*, if eighty musicians make good music, eight hundred must make ten times as good !

The scheme of wholesaling art proved profitable, and in 1872 another " Peace Festival" was arranged on much larger lines.   A hall holding fifty thousand people ; a chorus of twenty thousand members ; an orchestra of two thousand musicians ; a "bouquet of artists" consisting of fifty soloists who were to sing in unison or at times a dozen to a part ; a number of foreign bands ; a host of celebrated singers ; Strauss, the waltz-king ; fifty anvils, pounded by members of the Boston fire department in full uniform ; a battery of cannon to emphasise the rhythm of the " Star-spangled Banner ;" these were a few of the attractions offered at the musical bargain-counter. Yet American art was benefited by the "monster" (the word fits well) festivals; choristers came from every part of New England and the Middle States, and many a little singing school, or choir, or rustic chorus, that had been satisfied with singing the watery music of the cheap "Musical Convention" collections, was suddenly made acquainted with Handel, Haydn, Mozart, Beethoven, and other of the great masters. The classical musician might deplore some features of the colossal performances, but the fair-minded one will acknowledge that the Gilmore Peace Jubilees planted the seeds of good music in hundreds of villages where they had not existed before.

Gilmore wished for some special anthem which should be associated with the second festival, the largest musical gathering that had ever taken place on earth, and he found Matthias Keller's slow-moving theme, al-

though composed for war times, very well
suited to a celebration of peace. The typical American poet, Oliver Wendell Holmes,
was requested to change the sentiments of
the war-song.[1] It became a lofty theme
of reunion, in its new phase beginning :

"Angel of Peace, thou hast wandered too long!
Spread thy white wings to the sunshine of Love!
Come while our voices are blended in song, —
Fly to our ark, like the storm-beaten dove!
Speed o'er the far-sounding billows of song,
Crowned with thine olive-leaf garland of Love.
Angel of Peace, thou hast waited too long!"

Although even this song does not scale
the topmost heights of national music, it
may well stand as a type of what we hope
our country to be. It speaks of a united
nation and of a peaceful one; it is a song of
welcome to the suffering from every clime.

We may soon hope to possess a nobler
national hymn than any of those which are

[1] Keller died very poor, soon after his fame was established by the Peace Jubilee chorus.

described in these pages ; for, while America possessed no composers during the Revolution and the War of 1812, and no very great ones during the Civil War, she now may boast of a worthy band of native musical composers who shine in even the largest and severest forms of the art.

Paine, Chadwick, MacDowell, Strong, Foote, Buck, Parker, — the list might be extended to very large proportions. One of these composers will, some day, when the inspiration seizes him, possibly in the train of some great national events, bring forth the music of the true national hymn of America.

May God grant that the coming hymn be not born, as so many have been, in the midst of carnage and desolation ; may its music not be cradled in distress and baptised in blood! Yet it must not be wholly a song of peace either ; the trumpet must reverberate in its harmonies, the sacrifices which bought this country and made it what it is must not be forgotten in a sweet Lydian measure; and Liberty, though she should sleep, will readily reawaken at the sound of the national anthems of America.

THE END.

APPENDIX.

THROUGH the investigations of Mr. Frank Kidson, of London, Mr. W. B. Squire, of London, and Mr. Albert Matthews, of Boston, the author is enabled to add a few data to those collected in the body of this work. Dr. E. F. Rimbault, in an article in *Leisure Hour* (February, 1876), says that the tune of " Yankee Doodle " was handed to some American officers as a well-known piece of music, in 1755. Doctor Rimbault adds :

" We know that it was popular in England, and the tune was printed in one of Thomson's [*sic*] country-dancebooks as ' Kitty Fisher's Jig.' . . . We have a copy of Thomson's version of his tune which is written in triple time. It was afterward altered to common time as now known as ' Kitty Fisher's Jig.' "

On the foregoing, Mr. Frank Kidson, who is entitled to rank among the most earnest investigators of this troublesome subject, comments :

"I find no trace of 'Kitty Fisher's Jig' in any of Thompson's 'Country Dance Books.' There is a tune called 'Kitty Fisher' in 'Thompson's Dances' for 1760, but it is quite unlike the melody."

The author (for the sake of verification) appends this melody.

KITTY FISHER.

From "Thompson & Son's Twenty-four Country Dances, for 1760."

Doctor Rimbault's entire story seems apocryphal. Originally (in 1854) Doctor Rimbault asserted that he had found the tune "in 'Walsh's Collection of Dances for the year 1750,' where it is printed in ⅜ time, and called 'Fishers' Jig'" (*Historical Magazine*, July, 1858, II., 214). We give this melody as Doctor Rimbault printed it:

"KITTY FISHER'S JIG."

Leisure Hour, 1876, p. 90.

Since 1890, Mr. Kidson has found two copies of the Walsh book, and in neither is

there any air resembling "Yankee Doodle,"
or any tune called "Fisher's Jig." This should
certainly put the late Doctor Rimbault out
of the race as far as reliability is concerned.
He afterward changed his base to 'Thomson's
Collections,' but here, too, nothing has been
found to verify his statements.

The air on page 136 of this volume has
recently been more definitely traced. It was
published in 1782; it is, therefore, the earli
est known appearance of the melody in
print. We append it in full, with its quaint
variations.

YANKEE DOODLE.

From a selection of Scotch, English, Irish, and Foreign airs adapted to the violin, or German flute. Glasgow: printed and sold by James Aird. [No date, but according to Frank Kidson, Esq., 1782. Vol. I., p. 36, No. 102.]

Other early appearances of the tune are as follows :

YANKEE DOODLE.

From MS. book dated 1790, belonging to F. Kidson, Esq.

THE RETURN OF ULYSSES, TO ITHACA.

Allegretto.

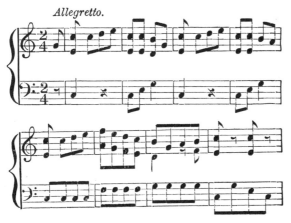

I sing U - lys - ses and those chiefs Who

out of near a mil-lion So luck-i - ly their

ba- con sav'd Be-fore the walls of Il - ion.

Yan - kee doo - dle, doo - dle, doo, Black

ne - gro he get fum - bo; And when you come to

our town We'll make you drunk with bum - bo.

Musical Tour of C. Dibdin, p. 342. 1788.

TWO TO ONE.

NEW COMIC OPERA COMPOSED BY DR. ARNOLD.

Ad-zooks, old crust - y, why so rust - y,

stu - pid, queer, and mump - y? E -

gad, if you don't mend your man - ners,

Somebod- y will lump you.

Lump - y, thump - y, thwack and bump,

Pum - mel you and bump. O l

Nump - y, stump - y, make you mump,

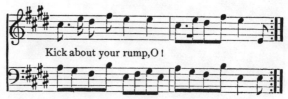

Kick about your rump,O !

London: Printed for Harrison & Co., No. 19 Paternoster Row. Published July 5, 1784.

INDEX.

———◆———

INDEX TO APPENDIX